ANTHONY ESOLEN

D0286957

# *How the Church Has Changed the World*

Publisher: Romain Lizé
Editor-in-Chief: Rev. Sebastian White, O.P.
Iconography: Isabelle Mascaras
Layout: Julia Pateu
Cover: Gauthier Delauné
Production: Florence Bellot
Proofreading: Janet Chevrier
Front cover: *Medieval city on the banks of a river* (detail),
Karl Friedrich Schinkel (1781-1841), Schloss Charlottenburg Art Museum, Berlin,
Germany. © akg-images.

Printed in April 2019 by Imprimerie Marquis, Canada
First edition: April 2019
Edition number: MGN19020
ISBN: 978-1-949239-04-1

ANTHONY ESOLEN

# *How the Church Has Changed the World*

Volume I

December 2013 – December 2015

MAGNIFICAT

Paris • New York • Oxford • Madrid • Warsaw

# CONTENTS

# FOREWORD

Professor Anthony Esolen is well known for the skill with which he wields his pen, as well as his passion for teaching the great treasures of Western civilization, especially those that find their roots in the Catholic Faith.

After several years of regular writing for MAGNIFICAT, with different themes and topics from year to year—from the sacraments to the Last Things, from liturgy to literature, including an entire year dedicated to Dante's *Divine Comedy*—in December of 2013 Professor Esolen began writing a new column, "How the Church Has Changed the World." It is a column he still writes, and which continues to garner the interest and appreciation of readers.

This volume, which comprises the first two years of that column, responds to a steady flow of requests to make his essays available again. They are back, as the saying goes, by popular demand.

In these twenty-five essays—which include the inspiring witness of priests, religious, and laity; which touch on the arts and sciences, civilian life and government, the realm of ideas and practical works of mercy—Professor Esolen displays how the Church is truly the "leaven and, as it were, the soul of human society in its renewal by Christ and transformation into the family of God" (*Gaudium et spes*, 40).

It is not uncommon to find books and articles presenting arguments that the Church has failed the world. Under Professor Esolen's tutelage, however, we will enjoy discovering how Holy Mother Church, as she leads us home to where all the angels and saints are gathered around the glorious throne of God, has indeed made our world a better place.

Rev. Sebastian White, o.p.
Editor-in-Chief, MAGNIFICAT
Yonkers, New York
Feast of Saints Philip and James, 2019

# A Child Enthroned

The Apennines run along the peninsula of Italy like a spine, carved and turned by volcanic action beneath the earth. So it is that abrupt cliffs of fire-founded rock rise up, smoothed a little by the long ages, pitted with grottoes, covered on their gentler western slopes with rich soil for farming, and crowned, often enough, by the walls and tile roofs and spires of a medieval town.

And here, in one such grotto, beyond the walls of one such town, a little man in brown rough cloth is working quietly. You wouldn't know it to look at him, but he has been in himself something of a volcano, if that word can properly apply to one who, by all appearances, hardly ever raises his voice. He is leading a great lumbering ox and a donkey over to the grotto, to tether them there, in front of a very large trough filled with hay so they won't grow restless, and a cistern full of water. The animals seem unusually tame, or maybe he just has a way with them.

## The church of the earth

Two other men in brown are watching him.

"Brother Rufino, what is the master doing now?" It's never been easy for the followers to

7

catch up with him. It is like trying to hold still the flashing points of a fire.

"I don't know. He said something about the chapel being too small."

"Too small for an ox and a donkey?"

"No, Brother Giles. Too small for the crowd that will come to celebrate the vigil with us."

Rufino and Giles approach the master. He is now strewing cedar branches and laurel along the sides of the grotto, as if he were decorating a stage. "My little brothers!" he cries out to them. "Come and assist me. Now is the time when what is great is small and what is small is great."

So they assist him, as if they were trying to transfigure a mountain and deck it as a sanctuary; as if the earth itself could now be a church once more, at the coming of the Lord who made it. At first they don't know what the task is, but after a while the plan takes shape in their minds too, and they pitch themselves into it with a will. The afternoon soon fades into evening, for the days are short, and in the waning light the people come, most especially children, some of whom the master dresses in white robes, giving them country horns and pipes to play with. Men and women come too, leading sheep, and a frisking lamb or two, just born this summer. Naturally, with the commotion come man's oldest and most loyal friends, the dogs, wagging their tails and barking, as the good Lord made them to do.

"Master," says Rufino, a man who was always a little too touchy about boundaries, "may we do this thing? Have we permission? What will the bishop say?" Rufino is the sort who, if he missed a word while saying his paternoster, would repeat the prayer three times over to make up for it. The master has had to correct him at times for that.

"The bishop of all the bishops has had his say. I have asked him, and he has approved. Brother Rufino," he says, his eyes glinting upon his friend, "when have you ever known me to take upon myself the burden of a priest? You know that my back is too weak to bear it."

## A new thing in the world

It is now quite dark above, a winter sky with stars like flakes of fire. The master leads a little girl and a little boy by the arm, and instructs them to kneel in front of the feeding trough, their hands folded in prayer. Then he brings a statue of an infant boy, which he had hidden for just this moment. He kisses its forehead, and falls to his knees.

All the people, hundreds of them, fall to their knees.

What can we hear, in that grotto on the slopes of Mount Subiaco? The earth is not trembling. Angels do not trumpet their songs from the skies. Some of the people are muttering a prayer, *Magnificat anima mea.* One of the lambs gives a shy bleat. The ox and the ass look on, padding now and then in their places, snuffling at the hay, or looking upon the people with their large expressive eyes.

Then the master arises to his feet, and begins to sing. *Puer nobis nascitur: A boy is born for us!*

Song after song, some in Latin, some in the Italian dialect of Umbria, rises up from the men and women and children, from the brothers in their coarse brown tunics, and from the angels surrounding the grotto, made all the lovelier by the occasional confusion of the animals, for they too partake of this glory. A few of the grandees of Assisi are present, but in this world, the real world, what is small is great and what is great is small, and not all their gay robes draw the eyes of the people as do the children in white, the ox and the ass and the sheep, the girl Mary and the boy Joseph, and the figure of the Holy Child.

Then, after the poetry of praise, and after a time of silence that even the dogs in their sagaciousness observe, the poor man of God, Francis Bernardone, steps before the people and preaches to them of the meaning of this night.

"This is a new thing in the world," he says. "This is perhaps the only new thing the world has ever seen." And he speaks to them of the Child in the manger. It is not only that God has deigned to come among us in so humble a guise. It is that he is instructing us even now. Even from the manger does Christ preach, saying, "If you would enter the kingdom of heaven, you must become as I am, you must become as little children." The child has nothing; the Son does nothing but what he sees the Father do. And therefore the Father has robed him in splendor.

"See the swaddling bands that wind him about," says the master. "Whose hands wove the cloth? It was Mary, in the quiet house in Nazareth, who wove those bands for the child she was going to bear, along with her dearest friend and my beloved, the Lady Poverty, and she and Mary spoke of many things as they worked, and no one but God beheld them."

So for an hour and more did Saint Francis preach, and the people there at the second crèche in the history of the world—for the first was at the stable-cave in Bethlehem—listened, as they always did, as if his clear and boyish voice swept them from that hillside into the land where the boy Christ looks upon his own, and makes the lion lie down with the lamb, and, more remarkable than that, the rich man to bow in homage to the poor, and leads them to streams of living water.

## The whole world a grotto

And in the rushing of Francis' words, the people for a time forget themselves. They forget to lift the chin and throw back the shoulders and strut like foolish peacocks in a cage. They forget to be great, and seem as if they had returned to childhood themselves, their eyes bright with delight and their lips parted in that happy look that children have when they are all wonder and no self. For the whole world, from the stars above to the rock beneath their feet, is a grotto for just this moment, to which the people have been invited, if they would but bow their heads and become small enough to fit into the universe.

The Evangelists tell us that the earth shook on the day when Christ died upon the cross. But that was the great after-tremor of Jesus' first act of love, when in the silence of Mary's house he became flesh and dwelt among us, and then, on the night of the Nativity, first showed to Mary and Joseph, then to the humble animals, and only then to mere shepherds, his sacred face. The earth shook with the fire of love, and from that day unto this, wherever men and women still remember the name of Jesus and how he was born in a lowly stable, they will feel that tremor, and know, somehow, even if they have forgotten the words, that the meek shall inherit the earth, that the first shall be last and the last shall be first, and that all the pomp and glamour of the world will pass away, all its capitols and senates and universities and towering dynamos of business leave not one scorched stone upon a stone, but the Child born in the manger will remain, and he alone can tell us the secret of who we are and where we must go.

ℰℐ ℰℐ ℰℐ

# THE PLAY'S THE THING

❧❧❧

**T**wo women are in the fields outside of Wakefield, tying bean seedlings to stakes. It's a clear and sunny day, with just enough of a breeze to bring to their ears the bass voice of a man, raving:

> *Heard I never quirk so quaint that a knave*
>     *so slight*
> *should come like a saint and rob me of my right!*
> *Nay without—nay without—refrain,*
>     *no—remain—restraint*
> *Nay without restraint, I shall kill him downright!*

"Dear me!" cries one of the women. "Are they brawling at the public house again?"

"Nay, not indeed," says the other, laughing. "It's my good husband, Will. He's playing Herod again this holiday. Twenty-two years has he done it, and still he will drop a rhyme or two, so he gives his lungs the airing whilst feeding the pigs."

"Ah, the mysteries! Fool that I am, I had forgotten. I hear that the brave lad of the Waters will be the Christ this year. He has not the look of a priest about him."

"Not if the bailey's daughter has anything to say about it! They are to be wed this Lammastide. But listen!"

*My guts will burst out*
*If I hang not this lout;*
*If my vengeance he flout,*
*    I may live no longer.*

"Aye, there's a voice of a man indeed! He does so enjoy playing that murdering rogue of a king."

"So long as the Lord not mistake him for Herod when he shall stand before him!"

### A shy creature, drama

I imagine such a conversation between two wives, in the little English village of Wakefield, in the merry old days of Catholic England. They're talking about their village plays for the three-day festival of Corpus Christi. It's something the people of Wakefield have known and loved for many generations.

We who go to the movies may suppose there's always been such a thing as drama. It isn't so. Drama is the most erratic of the arts, like a wild sweet fruit that grows only in a sheltered place, when the sun and rain are just right. They were just right in Athens, five centuries before Christ, when the old religion of Greece met a new thing called democracy, and the poets invented the play—meditations on man and the gods, complete with dance and song, and what we'd call a civic liturgy, to celebrate all that they revered as holy.

Conditions were right again when my mother was a little girl, when quite a few Catholics directed movies that were brilliant works of art. How did that happen? Men like John Ford and Frank Capra didn't graduate from film school. There wasn't any such. They had their hard education in human joy and suffering. They and their comrades knew what it was like to go down a coal mine, or sweat ten pounds a day in a foundry, or haul freight on the docks. They also knew what it was like to fall to their knees in worship. Even if they strayed from the Faith, they felt in their bones that only a holy day can ever really be a holiday. Back in my mother's time, there was a tiny theater on Main Street, called the Grand, a few blocks from the church, Saint Thomas Aquinas. I like to think that Thomas would have gone to a movie once in a while, especially if, as in *You Can't Take It with You*, we see love and merry folly defeat avarice and self-regard, or, as in *Sergeant York*, we see a humble and peace-loving farm boy become a hero in wartime, putting his life on the line for his fellows in the field.

But did Thomas ever see a play? Sure he did.

## A new holiday for an ancient truth

In 1215, at the Fourth Lateran Council, the Church re-affirmed the real presence of Christ in the Eucharist, Body, Blood, soul, and divinity. It was a cause for great rejoicing, and to mark the event, Pope Honorius declared a new holiday: Corpus Christi.

The feast was celebrated on the Thursday before Trinity Sunday. That was a deft theological move that Pope Honorius made. We were meant to think of the three great Thursdays in the history of salvation: the Thursday of the Lord's Supper, the Thursday of the Lord's Ascension, and now the Thursday of the Lord's presence among us in the sacrament of the altar, until the end of time. The feast was held for three days, too—echoing the three days commemorating Christ's Passion and Death, before the triumph of Easter. But these three concluded with the Sunday that celebrated the most profound mystery of God, that he is both One and a Communion of three Persons. Overnight the holiday became immensely popular. It didn't have the sweet merriment of Christmas, or the solemn joy of Easter. It had the boldness and breadth of summer days filled with light.

So, some priest, somewhere—call him Francisco Capra—got an idea. Why not celebrate the holiday by putting on stage the whole of the cosmos, the whole of the history of salvation? Not just one play, but a whole series of plays, rejoicing at the presence of Christ in the Eucharist and drawing near to the Blessed Trinity?

With the swiftness of a wildfire and the rush of a mighty stream, drama swept across Europe, and for once the slang held true, that everybody got in on the act. It wasn't professional. Each of a town's guilds would commit to the play nearest their hearts; so that the carpenters might stage the one about their hero, Noah the ark-builder. The plays would be performed on wheeled platforms, what we'd call floats, moving from station to station through the town, from chapel to chapel, over the three days. Imagine it! Fifteen or twenty or thirty plays, and who are the actors but your neighbors? Who built that "special effect" spring-action Gate of Hell that Christ bursts open with a finger-touch? You did. Who prepared the bread and meat and sweets for the crowds? You did. Who stood a-tiptoe in the audience, mouthing the words you knew your boy had to say, and laughing inside when he got them right? Who could sit at a fireside forty years later and recall with your friends the words of Jesus to Pilate, or how the big-bellied miller was "struck" in the forehead by the stone that David slung? You could do that, you and your neighbors, from Prague to Lisbon, from York to Rome, *for almost four hundred years.*

## What happened then

It was a rollicking, bumptious theater, smelling less of the schools than of the grocer's. Look at the plays from Wakefield. A sheep-stealer named Mak tries to "hide" his theft in a manger, pretending that his wife has given birth to a boy child in the night; while the true Lamb is born that same night nearby, as the good shepherds will see. Noah's got his ship all stocked, but he still can't budge the most reluctant creature to get into it while the rains are coming—Mrs. Noah. Your friends aren't fooled by any fussy limitations of time or space, so that a boy, cheering the defeat of Pharaoh and his charioteers, gives praise to "the Lord Emmanuel," as is right and just.

Many of these plays, from here, there, and everywhere, still survive, and we can see, behind the plain language and the popular stage action, a way of thinking about the world that informs the greatest Christian artists. We don't see time as a line from one point to another. All of salvation is reflected in each moment; the shadow of the cross falls upon the stable at Bethlehem; in the very curse upon Eve is the blessing that she will be the Mother of One who will crush the serpent's head.

Saint Thomas must have seen them when he was little, and his Grand Theater was the vault of the summer sky. But the greater drama to which he gave his heart, and for which he composed his own beautiful hymns, was the drama that the holiday commemorated. That drama was held every day, before every tabernacle in the world. We know its climax: FOR THIS IS MY BODY.

And when plays from classical Greece made their way west in the Renaissance, and when a new world was discovered hiding behind the western sea, poets didn't have to invent the drama all over again. They already had it, vibrant, popular, and deeply theological. The man of muscles was ready for action.

So the Church revived the drama, and gave the world the greatest dramatist who ever lived, a man from a Catholic family, who saw those rough and tumble plays when he was a boy, and learned from them, even as his poetry soared beyond what heights the villagers could attain.

That boy's name was William Shakespeare.

༐ ༐ ༐

# Raising a Nation
# from the Dead

※◦❀◦※

When Jesus came down from the mountain of the Transfiguration, he met a crowd with the rest of his disciples, surrounding a man whose son was possessed. The disciples had tried to cast out the spirit, but failed. And Jesus, disappointed by their weak faith, turned to the man and said, "If you can believe, all things are possible."

"Lord, I do believe," said the poor man, overcome by love and sorrow. "Please, help my unbelief."

Then Jesus rebuked the foul spirit, and when it departed it left the boy senseless upon the ground, as if dead. But Jesus raised the boy by the hand and led him home. There the disciples took Jesus aside and asked why they could not cast the spirit out.

"This kind," said Jesus, "comes out only by prayer and fasting."

## Life in the ruins

Father John treasured these words. They had been his anchor of hope. Not that there was much visible turmoil in the village to which he had been sent. It was not, there, as it had been in

Paris some years before, when the people rose up in revolt against their rulers, and then against the very leaders of their revolt, and runnels of blood ran fresh from the Place de la Concorde, as the national barber, the guillotine, did its swift and efficient work. For a while it seemed as though the very seasons had been sent to the scaffold, and men no longer could reckon time by the great works of God, but by foolish and ugly names invented by the new deities, names like the month of Thermidor. And in their madness they had removed the statue of the Blessed Mother from her cathedral and replaced her with a harlot to whom, without irony, they gave the name of Reason, and honored her as a goddess.

No, it was not like that here. In some ways it was worse. It was not the whirlwind. It was the wreckage after the whirlwind. The sun shone and the rain fell and the land yielded its fruit, and men and oxen worked the fields, and children ran about and got into trouble, but it was as if the village had been thrown to the ground by a deaf and dumb spirit. The church on Sunday was empty but for a few old widows in their black country lace. The miller cheated his customers, young men kept knives under their shirts, several men had taken women to their beds without bothering about marriage, every morning saw someone in a drunken sleep in a ditch; and far from the joy of the Faith, there was not even human mirth, but the hard cynical laughter of people who have given up on life. "Let us eat, drink, and be merry," they said, but their eyes were dull and their lips hard.

To this place, then, Father John had been sent. It seemed that the whole of France had heaved itself into apostasy, and what could one frail priest do about it?

"If you can believe," said Jesus to that desperate father, "all things are possible."

## A holy simplicity

Perhaps a more learned man would have been desperate. What could one simple man do against the witty slashes of Voltaire, who had cried out against the very Church to which he owed his humane education, *Ecrasez l'infâme! Tear down the unspeakable thing!* What could he do against the still deadlier poison of Rousseau, that urbane fellow who, having abandoned his own children, dared to write about the natural goodness of man, seeming to praise the teachings of Jesus while dismissing him to oblivion?

What could he do? Everywhere he turned, he found mockery. If he went to the city, some sour old revolutionary would spit upon his soutane, or some young epicure would do it, not out of spite, but from sheer boredom and irreligion. In the seminary it was little better. Father John had struggled for years over his lessons. He stammered. He knew what he thought, but his thoughts had the greatness and simplicity of a mountain; and it was hard to put a mountain into French words, let alone Latin. His fellow students and his teachers thought he was stupid.

"And I am stupid," he said to himself. "I must keep that always in mind. On my own I can think nothing true, say nothing that anyone will understand, and do nothing that will last."

But if John was often at a loss for words, it was for a reason which the other seminarians did not suspect. He was granted visions. They came to him after many miles of walking in the hills, and the earth seemed no longer earth but the paradise of God, and every moment was like a thousand years of his providing. At those times the greatest mind must gaze in stupor, in wonder. It was as when the brilliant Thomas said to his brother Reginald that he would write no more, because the grandeur of what he had witnessed made all that he had written seem as straw. John could hardly fight his way through a few pages of Thomas. Those were almost the only words of his that John really understood. But he understood them well.

To this village of Ars, then, he was sent, to be the Curé of Nowhere. He doubted he could win anyone over with rational argument, not because reason was his enemy, but because, when the people had lost their faith, they lost their reason too. They were like drunken men who argue for the sake of arguing. They had given over the quest for truth.

"This kind," said Jesus, "comes out only by prayer and fasting."

### Laboring in love

So that is exactly what Father John did. He retired to his small room. He prayed, he fasted. In doing so he immersed himself in the sufferings of the people of Ars. To pray for them, to fast for them, to beseech God to turn his privations to their blessing, was the most powerful form his charity assumed; and it flowed forth in many more visible acts of charity. He ate little, some days only a bit of bread, and yet that little sustained his wiry form, and he would go miles on foot to visit a sick old woman in the countryside, then back to the village for vespers, without rest; and eventually people noticed it.

It didn't happen right away. Jesus says that the kingdom of God is like a mustard seed. That seed is hard to see in space; it is also hard to see in time. Those first years at Ars, Father John fasted and prayed, he served his people in simple and unswerving duty. And, one person here and one person there, the church began to look more like a house of worshipers instead of a cavern; and they sat and heard him preach. How do you put a mountain into words? Father John still did not know how. He was not eloquent, yet the words came. The deaf and dumb spirit began to retreat.

### The people listened

For hours they listened. They heard the great elemental truths of the Christian faith, that God is holy, and man a sinner, and Christ came to suffer and to die for us, worthless as we are, because we are dearer to him than is all the rest of creation. Father John's devotion to the Blessed Sacrament was extraordinary. Helvetius and Diderot and all the others who mocked were dead and buried, but the Eucharist was still the one truly living thing in the world, because the Lord of life made himself present in it—God with us till the end of time. And when Father John Vianney raised the Host at the consecration, it seemed to the people—who now crowded the church so that there was hardly a spot left to kneel—that there never had been any moment but this, here.

Miracles came too, though John, overcome by the greater wonder, seemed never to be surprised by the lesser. Why should God not work healings to stun a *philosophe* into stony silence? Why should the Bread of heaven not provide a miraculous bounty in the granary during a famine? Why should God who searches our inmost hearts not whisper something of them to a poor confessor? And God did that; and a mighty river of visitors came to Ars, curious, despondent, zealous, guilty. And Father John Vianney heard their sins day and night, stopping to say Mass and the daily office, sometimes with hardly a break for food or sleep. He raised Catholic France from the dead.

Saint John Vianney is the patron of parish priests. He might well be the patron of all the faithful who dwell in a land of madness. I imagine him present at the base of the mountain of the Transfiguration, and a child called France is bound by a spirit that ties the tongue and stops up the ear, that keeps her from hearing the truth and speaking it. "Why could I not cast out the spirit?" he asks. We might ask the Lord the same question now.

"This kind," says Jesus, "only comes out by prayer and fasting."

℘ ℘ ℘

# X Man,
## Risen from the Dead

❧

**D**ionysius passed through the open door of his ancestral home, a modest structure of stone and wood situated beside a small stream in the village of Colonus. Old olive trees arched their boughs overhead, almost past bearing any fruit. Grapevines planted by Dionysius' grandfather's grandfather had matted two whole walls of the house with dark green. In the garden stood a small statue of Apollo, the god who shoots from afar, the god of healing, and so also the god who in Homer's *Iliad* sent a deadly plague among the Greeks for Agamemnon's brutish treatment of his priest. Dionysius knew many passages of that poem by heart, as any learned Greek would, though he and they hardly believed a word of them anymore.

Everywhere Dionysius turned, he saw the vestiges of a world that had been, and was no more. He looked up and saw, a few miles away, the jutting outcrop of the citadel of Athens, the Areopagus— the Hill of Ares, god of war. Dionysius shook his head. The god of war indeed. The god of war had long ago abandoned Athens, and now she was nothing but an appendage of the great empire of those disciplined, shrewd, and efficient louts, the Romans. Long ago, the free men of Athens had transacted their state affairs on that hill. That was where Pericles had delivered his funeral oration for the first casualties of the great war against Sparta and Thebes. But the plague arrived then, too, and soon Pericles was lost. Then the war was lost, then freedom was lost, and now it seemed that even being a Greek was lost.

And what did people climb the Hill of Ares to do now? They went there for the same sad reason why Dionysius, a judge of the court that met on that hill, had gone there today. They went there to pretend that they still had life in them. They went as intellectual shoppers at a bazaar, where all the idea-hucksters of the world stopped to sell their wares, magi from Persia, drug-toking mystics from India, would-be philosophers who claimed, though they were not certain about it, that we could not be certain about anything. And then the men would take sides, with noise and a show of passion but no real conviction. And then some would get drunk. And then they would go home, as Dionysius did.

## A new thing in the world

He sat down upon his couch, without saying a word. His wife, Calonice, came over to him, bringing him a small dish of dates and honey.

"My dear, you look as if the city had been destroyed!"

"Yes," he said, absently. "I think I have heard of the only really new thing in the world."

Then Dionysius recounted to her what had happened. It was a day like all others. Then a smallish ugly Jew with a hoarse voice, having waited his turn, ascended the portico to speak. A knot of Epicurean philosophers gathered at one side, they who believe that the world is a poor wreck of a place. They retreat from public service, and indeed from anything that might disrupt their days. Their great hope is not for joy, but for the absence of pain; a short life of philosophical chatter by the riverside, with the spring flowers in bloom, and some bread and cheese and oil and fruit. Their bodies may be young, but their spirits are old, and they have nowhere to go.

Another knot of philosophers gathered at the other side, the Stoics. They thrust themselves into public service, not because it brings them joy, but because it is their duty. They too hold the world in scorn. "Your son has died," someone might say to the staunch Stoic. "And when did I ever say he was immortal?" the Stoic was to reply. They too were old, and had nowhere to go.

Then the Jew began to speak.

## Saint Paul upon the Hill of Ares

"Men of Athens," he said, with a trace of irony, "I see you are religious people indeed! While I was walking about your city and looking at your objects of worship, I found one for every god imaginable. I even found an altar with this inscription: TO THE UNKNOWN GOD. So it seems that you do not know whom you worship—but I will reveal him to you.

"The God who made the world and everything in it is the Lord of heaven and earth. He does not dwell in man-made temples, nor does he need our service. Rather, he himself gives to all men their very life and breath and everything else. From one man he made all the nations spread abroad over the earth—even yours. He it was who brought them high and low, who made them great and small again." At that some of the Athenians glared; others looked to the ground.

"Why has he done so, you ask? So that they would seek him and reach out for him and find him! But he is not far from any one of us. For in him we live and move and have our being. One of your own lovers of wisdom has said so! And we are his children—so says one of your own poets.

"Men of Athens, it is time to give up your ignorance. Since we are the children of God, we should not think that he is like gold or silver or stone, which we have fashioned by our hands. It is time to turn toward the truth, and life! For God once overlooked that ignorance, but now he commands all men to repent. He has set a day when he will judge the world with justice, by the Man he has appointed—the Man whom he has raised from the dead."

"Raised from the dead!" cried a man from the audience, a follower of Plato. "You mean that his immortal spirit came to dwell in another form, perhaps in one of the heavenly bodies?"

"I mean no such thing," said the Jew. "I mean raised from the dead, in the flesh."

Laughter and mockery. For people who have grown old do not *really* wish to be made new.

"But I followed him," said Dionysius. "Light of my eyes," he said, taking his wife's hand in his, "I have invited him to our house. He is coming tonight."

### The old world is always passing away

Dionysius and his household welcomed Paul into their hearts. They welcomed Christ into their hearts. And this is a new thing in the world; the only really new thing the world has ever seen, and ever will see.

For the world of man is sometimes a pathetic ruin, and sometimes a glorious ruin, but always old, and passing into death and oblivion. Athens had fallen into the shadows. Babylon was but a name. The Roman Empire, so grand, was already riddled with termites; it was already like a great hulking engine, without a soul, and rotting within. Every single nation that has ever existed and that ever shall exist must pass away.

Man, on his own, has devised only two ways of confronting the age and death about him. One way is to pretend not to care, to cultivate the "virtue" of apathy, and to derive what pleasure one can from the hours remaining. The other way is to trust in a guiding providence, of vast power, but also distant from the human heart; to do one's duty, and resign oneself to whatever fate may bring. In neither of these ways is there any joy, or anything new.

Let Easter not grow "old" to us! Let us never lose the shock of that first morning of the new world, greater than the first morning when God saw the light and said that it was good! Nothing like Easter has ever occurred in the history of the world, or ever will—because it comes from outside of the world like an invader, to remake the world and man in it, like leaven in the lump, like a contagion of health, like youth spread by word of mouth and the laying on of hands.

The world without Easter is doddering. Nothing is solid; all is like a marble and gold façade over a yawning emptiness. With Easter, and, God help us, not some "spirit of Easter," not some foolish weakling revival of springtime, but the frighteningly real Resurrection of the flesh of Christ, the whole world is made new again. In Christ, even the Greece of Saint Dionysius the Areopagite, Bishop of Athens, lives. Even our own nations now can come to life again. Easter is not one day among the rest. It is the only day.

"Behold," said the One seated upon the throne, "I make all things new."

ભ ભ ભ

# Civilization in the Seed

❧

The warriors from the battlements of the Tyne fortress looked down in puzzlement. Every day there was more to see, more land cleared of rocks and stumps, the hole dug deeper for the foundation, more stones for building, and the men in coarse gray tunics, measuring the stones, cutting them with hammer and chisel, shaving them with two-man saws.

Those men were everywhere. They didn't speak much. They didn't swear the merry or filthy oaths of ordinary workmen. Their happiness was more unsettling than their silence. And then, at appointed hours, they gathered, and the sound of strange music, solemn even when most joyful, stole upon the ear. It seemed the low rumble of a mountain coming to life.

## Pagan no longer

"Aelfwin," said one to the other, "I don't understand the new ways. I'm a man whose hair is like snow, with seventy winters on my back." He clenched his right hand and held it up, regarding three jewel-set gold rings on his fingers. One of the rings showed a large dint, from the slash of a sword. Osbert's little finger was missing the last joint. "The lord gave me these when we set sail against the Swedes, and I cut down his ene-my from the side just when the wretch's mace was raised to kill him."

"I remember it well, Osbert. We had a fine feast that night. We slaughtered almost as many steers as Swedes, and the bench where I sat was still wet with Swedish blood, and the flagon I drank from had last touched the lips of the king's chief steward. It was a glorious night. The bard sang of it well."

"Nights like that pass by, and so do the bards, leaving us only the song. And the song never ends well! But warriors have always known that. We fight, our enemies fight, the vengeance comes, and we get what's coming to us, but for a time we live in glory. We gave some good knocks, didn't we, Aelfwin?"

"That we did. Nobody can take that away from us."

"Nobody but death can take that away. We knew the glory of victory, and we brought home the plunder, the rings and swords and golden cups and shields." Osbert fell silent for a moment. Somebody beside a cart was unloading a large flat object, bright with colors deeper than those of the rainbow. Osbert had seen glass before, but glass was clear.

"Where is it now, Aelfwin?" he said. "The lord we fought for is dead— that treacherous prince of the Swedelings slew him in his own hall, pretending to arrange a peace. He's dead, and we're old, and those men below us are building something, and I don't understand any of it."

"Yet you wear around your neck the cross of Christ."

"Yet I wear around my neck the cross of Christ. Our king wishes it, and I obey. I don't meddle with gods, Aelfwin. They had best be left to priests and kings. I'm just an old servant of our lord, and if he says, 'Wear this,' I wear it, and don't ask any questions. It's not for me to meddle with such things. I know my place."

## Changing the face of the land

Over to the east, in the flatlands a few miles from the sea, lay a shallow lake, long ago cut off from the coast by the working of the tides and the shifting sands. There were men at the lake, too. Some were heaping up earth to construct a dike through the middle of it, while others were digging a trench to drain away the water from one of two resulting ponds. Other men were digging other ditches for water to flow into the main, from a sunken waterlogged field here and there. You could almost hear the squelch of their feet. One or two men with mauls hacked away at alders and willows and other worthless shrubs that like the soaking.

"What are they going to do there?" asked Aelfwin.

"They say they are going to farm," said Osbert, and spat.

"They're going to farm in a marsh?"

"It won't be a marsh when they get through with it, you can be sure of that. Nobody learns a new trick in Ireland or France, but the abbot hears of it. He knows."

"Will there be cattle, too?"

"Yes, always, plenty of cattle, and plenty of work for men who live with cattle, and who spend their days digging up the mud with a plow behind a pair of oxen. Plenty to do. This place will be rich, Aelfwin my friend. You take my word for it. There's one thing about it that I do understand. It's the only thing a soldier could understand. They obey. They will get a lot done. It's the only way to get anything done."

And in fact, though the vista beneath them was filled with men employed at quite a variety of tasks, no one seemed hurried, and there was no disorder. Then a bell tolled. It was the hour of none. The men in the fields paused in their work. The two old warriors bowed their heads. A clear tenor rang out, *Angelus Domini nuntiavit Mariae*. The warriors knew what that meant. It meant something holy.

## Christ comes to the northmen

They had been baptized, of course. They had learned the story of Mary, and how the angel came to her and declared that she would bear the Son of God; and from his great hall in heaven, where the angels and the holy ones sing and the mead flows freely, and the sway of the harp is heard from one great towering wall to the other, with the laughter of men and women and boys and blissful maidens, from that great hall came, as a little child, the warrior Christ. And he was born in a trough for watering cows and horses, but not forever was his royalty hidden, no, not when he did battle against Satan on the Hill of Calvary, and defeated that giant, and sent him down to exile into the hollows of the earth, to bemoan the glory he had lost and never to sing again. And Osbert recalled the instruction he had gotten from Brother Aidan, who clapped him on the shoulder with a plowman's hand and half said, half sang,

> He won that battle against the boaster—
>    showed who was the best fighter!
> With no sword, with no shield,
>    but with His sole courage,
> His manhood and mind-strength,
>    He mastered that traitor,
> To Hell sent him hasting—Heaven's bliss is
>    the greater—

*To cleanse this creation, clotted with sin,*
*And make fair and free the fire of man's soul.*

The cantor's voice rang again, *Et Verbum caro factum est*. Osbert hadn't any guess as to what that meant, but he fingered the cross about his neck, and said the prayer that his instructor had taught him, about Mary and sinners and death.

There was a time, in his youth, when he'd have bristled at the touch of a plowman, he, the pommel upon the lord's sword! But that was long ago. Brother Aidan had died since, and was buried in the little plot of ground beside the chapel. When he died, Osbert went to Mass to pray for his soul. He was surrounded by the monks, some of whom cast a sidelong glance at his armor, while others paid him no mind but went about their more important business. That night, after the burial, they invited Osbert to their table, where they ate black bread with cheese and roasted chickens and greens from the kitchen garden, and drank beer almost as dark and thick as the bread. That was a good meal, and somehow, Osbert could never quite tell how, he, the burly warrior, his face and arms scarred with fighting, felt as sheepish and happy as a boy whom his father welcomes for the first time to sit and sup with the grown men.

No," said Osbert again, "I'm too old to figure these things out."

## Our task

The monastery in Jarrow, on the River Tyne, facing the North Sea and the Vikings beyond it, became the greatest center of learning in the British Isles. Saint Bede the Venerable would live there, and write, among his theological works, his *Ecclesiastical History of the English People*, from which we learn not only about England but about the missionary drive of the Church all over the continent during the centuries following the fall of the Roman Empire in the West.

What happened at Jarrow had happened and would happen everywhere. The monks, wherever they went, brought light. They drained the swamps, they cleared the thickets, they built mills, they turned bad land into good, and they introduced an orderly and productive way of life. Where there had been but warring pagan tribes, living the half-settled lives of part-time herders and part-time marauders, they built their monasteries, which became the seeds of free Christian towns. They made *Europe*, and brought Europe to Christ.

Their double task is ours again. Our wilderness is of the intellect and the heart, but we have their example to guide us, and the battle cry of the only true Lord, our leader in the vanguard, who comes to baptize the world with the Holy Spirit and fire.

# In Praise of Woman

❦

The boy Adeodatus sat near the window, looking out to the west and the setting sun. Ostia was still humming with business, now mingled with the chatter of women going home from the bakers and the hawkers of greens and fruit and oil. He could make out the sharp clean smell of the resin and pitch from the Street of the Shipwrights, but now there was also that other air, the one he always associated with a woman, the sweet air of fresh bread and olives, the smell of the hearth and of its strong and quiet life.

"*Fili mi,*" said his father, approaching him from behind and laying a hand upon his shoulder. "What are you thinking of?" But he knew well what the boy was thinking of.

A month ago, in this room, his mother, the boy's grandmother, had died. Several friends were there too. They owed their lives to that woman. Not the running of the blood in the veins, but the breathing of the Spirit of God in their souls. She had brought him, her wayward son Augustine, to the Faith; she had seen the fulfillment of her years of prayer and weeping. He was baptized in the water of her tears.

Then there came a day when she was preparing to return to her native land, in Africa. Or so it seemed; and they stood at this same window, she and Augustine, and could smell the tang of the salt air from the ocean beyond the public buildings and the amphitheater and the merchants' shops and the trees, the stray dogs and the birds and the things of the passing hours. And then they spoke about the years they had seen, in Thagaste, in Carthage, in Milan, and now in Rome and this port of Rome; their wandering, their sorrow, his flight from her care, her steadfastness in pursuit, the wise and holy bishop Ambrose, and the mercy of God, more persistent and more fearful than any army, and sweeter for the defeated soul than any victory on earth could be. And their minds were lifted up from the passing day to the eternal, as they stood together for the last time on earth, mother and son, child of God and child of God.

A few days later, she caught a fever. It was not the ship to Africa that she boarded. Her homeland was not there. When she took her last breath, Adeodatus burst into tears, still at that age where the man within wrestles with the boy. Augustine rebuked him, and Adeodatus regained control of himself, understanding that it was not a time for the Christian to weep, unless they were tears of quiet gratitude.

## Why born of a woman?

"Father," said Adeodatus, "why was the Christ born of a woman?"

"Why, how else should he have been born?" Augustine made the jest to win some time. The boy was remarkably quick and perceptive, he thought, and would someday exceed his father in learning and literary accomplishment.

"I know that," said Adeodatus, turning to his father with an agreeable smile, but not willing to give up the point. "What I mean is not so much that he was born of a woman, but that, seeing that he would have to be born of a woman, why he would choose to come among us in that way. For he could have come among us in a different way."

"Son," said Augustine, "you must not despise matter. That was the error of those pestilent Manicheans, the error that led me wrong for so long a time. All of this creation is good; God declared it so in the beginning. So too then is it good to be born of a woman, to take on human flesh, to dwell among us as a man like us in all things but sin, as the Apostle says. He is our brother, truly."

"What I mean is this, Father." Adeodatus struggled to put his thought into words. "The woman is weaker than the man. She can't rig a ship or plow a field or fight a battle. But the Lord born in the manger was the weakest of all, and so too the Lord upon the cross. And his Mother was the one person in the world who was there both when he was born and when he died. And the Lord said, too, that the first shall be last and the last shall be first, and that he who exalts himself shall be humbled, and he who humbles himself shall be exalted."

"Go on," said the proud father, "come to your conclusion."

"I conclude that it was a humbling thing and an exalting thing. It was the humblest thing of all for the Christ to be born of a woman, and an exalting thing for the woman, and for all women." He turned back to the window and gestured toward the Street of the Shipwrights. "Is that the true world, Father, that world where men fight and conquer, buy and sell, build and destroy?"

"You know the answer to that already, my son." He sat beside him and looked out of the window. "You're thinking of your grandmother."

"Yes, Father."

### Where greatness is to be found

The sun was down, and the noise of labor had ceased. Now came the friendly calls of neighbors to one another, men and women, and the sing-song play of children, with a dog barking, and the thrushes in the coverts trilling their farewell to the day. "Father," said Adeodatus, "I've read that when Pericles of Athens made his oration at the funeral of the first fallen soldiers in the great war with Lacedaemon, he said about the women of Athens that their highest praise was that nobody had anything to say about them at all, good or ill."

"Yes, son, the Athenian women mainly kept to their household work."

"Then they were not great enough to be spoken of?"

"Perhaps not, my son."

"Was grandmother great enough to be spoken of?"

Augustine laughed. "Son, what would she have said to that, if she were here? I'm sure she would have given you a cuff to the head!" Augustine pitched and rasped his voice, like an old woman's. "What sort of nonsense does your father have you reading in those pagan books? Me, great? Go get us some firewood and make use of yourself, before some bird comes while you're daydreaming and pecks away what little brains you have left!"

Adeodatus picked up the play. "And you watch out, or you'll end up as wooden-headed as your father!"

They laughed and fell silent. "Yes," said Augustine, "she was great enough to be spoken of."

"Will you speak of her, Father?"

Augustine considered for a moment. There were accounts of women martyrs, like Perpetua and Felicity, like Lucy and Anastasia; but they had shown manly virtue in trials to the death. And then the Sacred Scriptures were filled with accounts of holy women, like Ruth and Esther and Judith, and the Mother of the Lord, Mary. But had anyone ever written of an ordinary woman, like his own mother? There were love poems, but that was different. A man might praise his mistress, as Catullus did, and then write scabrous verses in anger against her. Then there was the legendary Lucretia, whose claim to renown was that she was ravished, and after she swore her husband and his friends to vengeance, she slew herself. No one had ever written an account of the life of a woman before. His mother was not the head of a noble family, like Cornelia. She hadn't whored her way into political intrigues, like Cleopatra. She could not even read. She was only a woman.

"Yes, my son, someday I will, I promise you."

## A new thing in the world

And that is what Saint Augustine did, in his *Confessions*. He devoted a long chapter to the biography of his mother, Saint Monica. He told of her birth, her habits as a child, her marriage with the worldly Patricius, her love for husband and son, her strength of soul, her meekness, her perseverance, the depth of her faith—even her foibles; he wrote about her what no man had ever written about any woman before, and she was a woman to whose like the world had never given a passing thought.

Saint Paul said, "In Christ there is neither man nor woman, neither slave nor free," and that did not mean that it was of no importance whether one was a man or a woman. The very Incarnation ruled out any dismissive contempt for the fact of sex. It meant that the woman shared equally with the man in the life of Christ. It meant, for the first time in the world, that an ordinary sinner of a man might admire the extraordinary virtue of a good woman, even his own mother or his wife. It did not mean anything about rulership—for the woman who ceases to be a woman inverts the promise of Jesus, and seeks exaltation in and from herself. Augustine saw it, not by his own power of intellect and not by his natural predilection, but by the force of the Gospel and by the example of his mother.

The life of a woman—who in that old world would have guessed?

ᕬ ᕬ ᕬ

# WHATSOEVER YOU DO

᠊ᥱᥱ᠌ᥱᥱ᠌ᥩᡭᥣᥩᥱᥱᥱᥱ᠊

**O**ne day, as Jesus was entering Capernaum in Galilee, a Roman centurion sent for him, and pleaded with him to heal his dying servant whom he dearly loved.

The Jewish elders joined in the plea, because this centurion was a friend of the Jews. He may have been, in his heart, a convert to the faith in the one God. "He loves our nation," they said, "and has built a synagogue for us!" Seeming to take no note of that reason, Jesus approaches the centurion's house, but the centurion, abashed because he knows that he is a pagan and a sinner, says, "Lord, I am not worthy that you should enter under my roof, but only say the word, and my servant shall be healed."

Jesus marvels, saying, "I have not found such faith in all of Israel!" And the servant was healed from that moment.

But the scene prompts a question. The centurion is rich enough to build a synagogue at his own expense. He lives in the bustling town of Capernaum, on the north shore of the Sea of Galilee; and the new Roman city of Caesarea Philippi is not far away. Why hasn't he brought his servant to the hospital?

You will answer, "Because there were no hospitals in those days," and you will be right, in part. There were health resorts, often built up around natural hot springs in those lands perched atop the volcanic ring of fire. Wherever the Romans found hot springs, they built resorts, even as far north as England: *Bath*. But there was no such thing as a hospital, where you could go if you were ill and needed care and were not rich enough to get to the spas, and had no money to hire the learned physicians. Apparently there was nowhere to go in Capernaum, even for a centurion with means.

And that prompts another question: "Why were there no hospitals?" It cannot be for want of funds. The Romans were energetic at public works, and when their armies were not busy fighting, they were employed as a corps of engineers and construction workers, building aqueducts, theaters, the civic halls we know as basilicas, temples, roads, and bridges. They could have built hospitals also. Nor was it for want of medical knowledge. The Greeks had learned medicine from the traditions of the Egyptians, whose accumulated knowledge spanned two thousand years. The Greek Hippocrates had bequeathed to the world the oath that bears his name, enjoining a sacred code upon all physicians. "The art takes a long time to learn," said Hippocrates, "and life is short." Those are not the words of a quack.

So why were there no hospitals, for anyone and everyone? Because Jesus had yet to give mankind, through his Church, the great directive. "I was sick, and you visited me," says the Lord at the final judgment, and when the righteous reply, "But Lord, we never saw you sick," the answer comes, "Whatsoever you do to the least of these my brothers, the same have you done unto me." Every human being is of inestimable worth; not because he is rich or powerful, or dear to someone who is rich or powerful. Christians are commanded to see in the face of every human being the face of their brother—the face of Jesus. That transforms the world.

What do we suppose the Christians built, soon after Constantine issued the Edict of Milan in 313, legalizing Christian worship throughout the Roman Empire? They built churches, of course; and hospitals were not far behind. Saint Basil, the great theologian and Bishop of Cappadocia, founded an enormous complex of buildings and streets just outside of his city of Caesarea for the care of the sick. It was so large, it came to be called the New Town. There were buildings for different kinds of patients, a home for infants, a home for the aged, and a lazaretto for people afflicted with contagious diseases. There were dwellings for physicians and nurses, so they could be always near the people they were treating. There were even workshops and schools where men crippled by disease or injury might learn a trade, to support themselves and their families.

It wasn't the only such place. In Constantinople alone, during the reign of Justinian, there were thirty-five hospital foundations. In the Middle Ages, religious orders were established, such as the Knights Hospitalers of Saint John, whose vocation was to care for strangers and pilgrims and the sick. Wherever they went, they were bound by vow to build a hospital. When, in the 13th century, town life returned to Europe with great vigor (for the Vikings and other Germanic and Slavic pagans had been converted to Christianity, and no longer made life on the borderlands or on the seacoasts precarious), new hospitals were founded everywhere, so that in Germany every small town of five thousand persons had its hospital. Pope Innocent III himself commissioned the construction of the Santo Spirito hospital, near the Vatican, hiring a hospital architect from France to do the job; and when bishops from other parts of the world came to the Vatican, Innocent urged them to visit the Santo Spirito and to go back home and build hospitals on that model.

And that prompts still another question: "What was the model for a hospital?" We are apt to think that the places must have been dim, miserable, and filthy, where nobody but beggars and desperate men would go. Such is the residue of the prejudice against the Middle Ages engrained in us, who are instructed to fall in worship of new things because they are new.

There's no doubt that medical science can accomplish things that would stun the beholder with wonder—not just a medieval man, but even someone from the days of our grandparents. But that's no reason to suppose that the Church did not do her utmost, in the hospitals, to cure disease, and to comfort the dying, according to the best medical knowledge then available. And more: in some ways the hospitals the Church built were superior to ours.

Sometimes I believe that the evil attraction to euthanasia arises from a natural horror of hospitals such as they are. When my wife's mother was dying, we stayed with her at the hospital for several days, in the white, sterile, impersonal room, hearing the blips of the machines, the drone of the television, and the calls on the intercom. The doctors and nurses were quite efficient—one might say, coldly and mechanically efficient. Of course, since she was going to die, they wanted her to do it as soon as possible, with as little trouble as possible to anybody else, and to that effect they wanted to prescribe morphine, even though she was in no pain. We told them to keep their morphine to themselves. After a few days, though they did not need the bed, and though it could only harm my mother-in-law, they ordered her removed to a local hospice, where she soon died.

It is hard for us to imagine, but the Church built hospitals that were *beautiful*. Well, these were medieval men, who had not yet acquired the modern knack of building things intended to be ugly; every chance they had, they surrounded themselves with things of beauty. But they also believed that a sick or dying person above all should be comforted with beauty. They built lovely hospitals, usually outside of the town walls, for fresher air. It was the custom, says Dr. James Walsh in *The World's Debt to the Catholic Church*, "to decorate the hospitals with beautiful frescoes and the result was that patients had much more occupation of mind than they have in our bare walled hospitals." Imagine that you are lying on the bed from which you will not rise, and seeing, near to you in more ways than one, a painting of *The Mystical Marriage of Saint Catherine*, with the Christ Child enthroned in the bosom of Mary, placing a golden ring upon the finger of that young saint who suffered so much in her body as she prayed and labored for the welfare of the Church.

I'm not making that up. That is what you might have seen if you lay in the Hospital of Saint John, in Bruges. And it was no local child they hired to decorate the walls with some garish cartoon. It was the exquisite Hans Memmling, who knew how to make the countenance of a holy woman like that of a queen. If you were not in Bruges, but in the Hospital of Charity in Seville, you would have seen the work of Murillo, the kindly and gentle genius. Perhaps you'd have seen his *Return of the Prodigal Son*, with the old father embracing the poor bedraggled lad, while a small white dog, tail held high, leaps up to greet him.

For the Christians who built these hospitals never forgot that man has a soul as well as a body, and that he longs to leave his bed of illness to return to one home, or to another.

# The Church,
## the Ennobler of Cultures

❧❧❧

The cattle keepers had done with their day's labor, and were now noisily gathering in one of the halls on the monastery grounds. It was a feast day, and that meant a celebration, not with wine, since it was too far north for grapevines, and what wine the good abbess Hilda kept was for the Sacrament and for visitors. They'd be drinking beer, good dark stuff with the smell and the smack of the grain that grew in the fields of Whitby.

Caedmon knew what else it meant. There's no such thing as a feast without song, and no festal song without praise of gods and the heroes of old. So his father had sung tales of Sigemund and Ingeld, and his grandfather, and men going back countless generations, even to the days when giants roamed the earth. Caedmon loved with a guilty love the tales of the heroes and their wars with giants and dragons, and of their enmities and feuds. In those northern lands, where winter is long and dark, it seemed that the noblest of the heroes ended their days in defeat, but bravely fighting on to the last, strongest in will when their weary arms could hardly lift a sword.

They stirred something at once bitter and enticing in Caedmon's heart. His hand reached toward the wooden cross about his neck. And the men were silent while one of their fellows swept his fingers across the harp and sang of the demigod Weland the Blacksmith. And when he ended his song they shouted like boys, and the harp made its way around the table, each man in turn to sing one of the old songs, while the beer flowed freely.

"Good brothers," Caedmon said, rising from the table, "it's my turn to see to the cows tonight," and he left, alone, for the stables.

## Do not destroy, but purify

Caedmon didn't know it, but over a hundred years ago a ship filled with northern prisoners of war put in at Rome, and there a man named Gregory beheld those young Saxons, tall and blond. "Who are these people?" Gregory asked.

"*Sunt Angli*," the trader replied. "They are Angles."

"*Non Angli sed angeli*," said Gregory: not Angles, but angels. When Gregory became pope, he sent missionaries to the British Isles to bring the Gospel of Christ to those pagans. Saint Augustine, first Bishop of Canterbury, was one of them. Augustine was a careful man, to whom Gregory sometimes needed to give gentle encouragement.

The pagan Angles and Saxons were rough customers. They had the virtues and the shortcomings of a warrior society; courageous, intransigent, grudge-holding, heedless of the future, fiercely loyal, even while their poetry was filled with tales of treachery. They worshiped their gods, and their shrines were stained with the rusty brown of immemorial human blood.

Augustine trusted Gregory's judgment more than he trusted his own. "What shall be done with the pagan shrines?" he wrote to the pope. "Shall we destroy them?" That seemed the obvious course of action.

So Gregory prayed for wisdom.

It wasn't simply a matter of the shrine, but of everything the shrine represented, the whole of that pagan life lived under the darkness of sin and error, even the wickedness of human sacrifice. Why should any of it be preserved? Yet Gregory thought of the strange domed temple to all the pagan gods, the Pantheon, now a church dedicated to all the saints. There was an opening in that dome at the top through which the sun in its circling would shed light upon each of the twelve gods—now each of twelve saints. The darkness of the pagan world was great, but not total. God had left sinful mankind to the vanity of his imagination, and man had changed the glory of the incorruptible God, as Saint Paul put it, into an image of corruptible man, or of birds and beasts and creatures that slither upon the ground. And yet man still longed for the true God in his heart.

"Do not destroy the shrines," Gregory wrote back to Augustine, "but purify them, and rededicate them to Christ."

## "Sing me something"

What happened to Caedmon that night? Bede the Venerable tells the story:

At the proper hour he laid his limbs to rest and fell asleep. Then a man stood before him in a dream and hailed him, greeting him by name. "Caedmon!" he called out. "Sing me something."

Then Caedmon replied, "I don't know anything to sing, and that's why I left the beer-feast and came here—because I don't know how to sing."

"Nevertheless, you can sing."

"What shall I sing?"

"Sing me *frumsceaft*," said the man: Sing me the First-Making.

When Caedmon received this reply he began, in praise of God's creation, to sing verses and words he had never heard before, whose order is as follows:

*"Now let us laud    the Lord of heaven's realm,*
*the Measurer's might    and his mind-plan,*

> *work of the Glory-Father     as every wondrous thing,*
> *Chieftain eternal,     he established from of old.*
> *He first shaped,     for the sons of earth,*
> *the high roof of heaven,     holy Creator;*
> *the middle-yard     mankind's Lord,*
> *Chieftain eternal,     adorned after that,*
> *made the earth for men,     the Master almighty."*

Then he rose from his sleep and committed to memory all that he had sung while sleeping, and to those words in the same fashion he added many other words worthy of a hymn to God.

It isn't often that a man, visited by a herald of God, composes glorious poetry in his dreams. Caedmon told his foreman about it, and he in turn brought Caedmon before the abbess Hilda, who called the elders about her to advise her in the matter. She instructed them to read to Caedmon one of the narratives from Scripture, to see what he could do with it, and when Caedmon returned on the morrow, singing the same story in the ancient meter of the heroic lays, Hilda rejoiced, and they all concluded that Caedmon had been blessed with a rare gift from God. She invited Caedmon to leave the secular life and join them at the monastery.

So the very poetry that Caedmon could not sing at the beer-feast became the foundation for a new thing in the world—poetry of an ancient and pagan form, steeped in centuries of tradition, not destroyed but purified, built up into a shrine in honor of the great warriors Abraham and Moses and the Apostles, who served the true and only Lord, the God and Father of Jesus Christ. For the monks continued to read to Caedmon, and he, who could not read, transformed all that he heard into beautiful and virtue-inspiring poetry, and the monks wrote it down. They did this until the day the meek old man laid down his life in the infirmary, after asking for the Eucharist, making his peace with his friends, and turning his ear toward the dawn-song, as the monks in the chapel rose for lauds.

## Baptize all nations

What happened at Whitby is a model for what the Church's missionaries have ever done. Grace does not supplant nature, but perfects it. To enter the Church is not to lose one's culture, but to raise it up—sometimes even from the dead. When our Lady appeared to Juan Diego at Guadalupe, it wasn't as a European, but as a native princess. When Matteo Ricci traveled to China to evangelize, he steeped himself in the wisdom of the Chinese; he became a mandarin, to convert the mandarins. When Junípero Serra established his missions in California, he brought to the natives what for them were new tools, such as the millstone and the waterwheel and the winepress, and the cultivation of the grape, the olive, and other foods. It wasn't to make them European, but to make them self-sufficient, strong enough to resist the depredations of bad men. The mission churches were like the poetry of Caedmon, native ways raised up in honor of Christ.

This has been the Church's way. The world confuses unity with uniformity, and charges the Church with doing what the world does—for the powers of the world can't bear contradiction, so they attempt to compel people to obey their will in their fashion at their command and in their time. Wherever the Christless modern rulers go, they reduce things to one homogeneous mass.

But Christ didn't say, "Go and form all nations into one." He said, "Go forth unto all nations, baptizing them in the name of the Father, and of the Son, and of the Holy Spirit." And when the people assembled in Jerusalem for the feast of Pentecost and heard the Apostles preaching, it wasn't all in the *same* language, but each in his *own* language, so that, if the cowherd Caedmon had been there, he'd have heard it in Anglo-Saxon, filled with the life of all that was good and noble in that culture.

For that's exactly what did happen, in that stable in Whitby, long ago.

&#8531; &#8531; &#8531;

# THE POET IN LOVE
## WITH THE WORD

⁕

The young Jesuit had been sent to the northern mountains of Wales, of all places. "What am I doing here?" he asked himself as he walked along the muddy roads about the village. The ready answer was that he was studying theology at the Jesuit school at Saint Beuno's. But that hardly satisfied. So he often went wandering alone outdoors, for many hours, despite his small stature and his frail health.

Some people when they walk and think see only with the inward eye, lost in speculations. Such a man was Thomas Aquinas, whose power of concentration was so intense that he seemed sometimes to forget where he was and who was beside him. One day, at table with the lords and ladies of the court of the saintly King Louis, Thomas banged his ox's fist on the table and bellowed, "Thus are the Manicheans refuted!"

"Boy," said the King to a page nearby, "fetch Brother Thomas some ink and paper."

Father Hopkins was not like Thomas. In fact, he was engaged in a friendly quarrel with Thomas' philosophy. Thomas had affirmed the reality of *kinds* of things, universals, which we can come to know when we perceive individual things through our senses. But John the Scot, the Subtle Doctor, argued that Thomas hadn't given sufficient status to those individual things. They too, he said, possessed an essence unique to each creature, a *this*-ness, as the Scot put it, straining language to the utmost to express a thought so difficult to specify and so easy to misunderstand.

### "What I do is me: for this I came!"

So the priest, this devotee of Blessed Scotus, was all eye and ear as he walked, his senses awake and keen. Mount Snowden, the highest peak in Wales, rose in the distance, but Father Hopkins didn't need to seek out the picturesque. People who do that are like those who throng about celebrity, and miss the real, solid, and mysterious goodness and beauty of those who are near to them; the blacksmith with his hammer shooting sparks from the horseshoe against the anvil; the bugler from the army regiment, fresh-faced and still more boy than man, asking Father about the Faith; the boys and girls crowning Mary with flowers…. The world was almost too rich for one heart to bear it.

He gazed at a farm alongside the road. There was a man working the land. The oxen, tame, patient, sad-eyed beasts, set their hooves in the mud and strained, while the man directed the harrow behind them, turning up clods of good black earth, glossy in the sunshine. What an odd tool that many-tined harrow was; or the hoe, or the spade, or the fork for the hay, or the sickle for reaping, or the flail for threshing and the fan for the winnowing floor. Each of these things cried out, "Behold me!" *And all trades,* thought the priest, *their gear and their tackle and trim.*

He looked at a clump of cornflowers, those sprightly weeds, and stood stock-still for a few minutes. It was as if he were painting them—he was an artist, too, from a large and artistic family. Or rather they were painting themselves upon his soul, with a power that came from deep within them, a power he called *instress,* to reveal the handiwork of God. People don't understand what it means, he thought, when they say, "I believe in God, the Father Almighty, Creator of heaven and earth." It didn't mean that God created things long ago and had done with them. None of the Church Fathers believed so foolish a thing. It is God himself who creates now, veining the green stalks of the cornflowers, and causing their petals to burst out in so brave a display of dusky blue. This was no flight of imagination. It was the plain fact, as sweet and homely as the wet ruts that the plowman was leaving behind him in his work.

## The Word of God and the word of man

Other priests, impatient with the rural ways of these Welsh miners and farmers, would have missed the beauty of that mud, but Father Hopkins did not. As burdened as he was with study and teaching, he'd set himself to learn Welsh, that odd language, gruff and liquid by turns, that seemed made for the men's choirs that sang in it so well. He traded words in Welsh with the faithful at Saint Beuno's. He had learned to sing old Welsh songs. He had caught the Welsh knack of playing rhymes all over the words, not just at the end. He'd even composed a few poems of his own in Welsh.

But these Welsh words above all rang in his soul: *Yn y dechreuad yr oedd y Gair, a'r Gair oedd gyd a Duw, a Duw oedd y Gair: In the beginning was the Word, and the Word was with God, and the Word was God.* And the Word, through Whom all things were made, dwelt among us in the world, to be found in the essence he, the master artist, had instilled into each thing. Father Hopkins called it their *inscape.* Some people looked for God and saw the world instead. Hopkins saw the Word at work in and through the world; everything in the world was meant to turn his heart to Christ. Most of all: other men, each in his marvelous unrepeatable individuality. What did Jesus look like? Where are the resemblances? In that plowman at the furrows, in his sturdy wife calling him in for supper, in the child hanging from the willow branch by the cistern: *Christ plays in ten thousand places.*

For some years, he had given up writing poems as a distraction from his priestly vocation, but now he was working out in his mind the revival of something at the heart of all poetry. Just as each created thing—the cornflowers, the clouds drifting like grain in the sieve, the violet of Mount Snowden in the evening sun—was a word spoken by God, so too man may speak words that honor the Word and the world that God made. The poet's task was to see the Word of God in the world, and to impress into his words what he had seen, handling the words like mysterious things, living, containing hidden springs and light, surprising, dangerous. The result was poetry unlike what the public were accustomed to, Father Hopkins knew; his lot was to be unread or misunderstood.

## "Rhine refused them; Thames would ruin them"

But his superior had assigned him a task. The despisers of the Church in Germany, under Otto von Bismarck, were waging the *Kulturkampf,* a relentless cultural war against the Faith. Last winter, five Franciscan nuns had fled the persecution, sailing to England on the *Deutschland*. A terrible snowstorm, as if in the dark providence of God, had destroyed the ship just off the Kentish knock. The Mother Superior stood tall upon the deck, heartening her sisters and crying out, "Come quickly, come quickly, O Christ!" Fifty-seven people died, including all of the sisters. Father Hopkins was to honor these martyred women in verse.

To this task then Gerard Manley Hopkins set himself, and the first stanza, rugged, strange, filled with words bursting into meanings beyond his full control, came to him:

> *THOU mastering me*
> *God! giver of breath and bread;*
> *World's strand, sway of the sea;*
> *Lord of living and dead;*
> *Thou hast bound bones and veins in me,*
> *    fastened me flesh,*
> *And after it almost unmade, what with dread,*
> *Thy doing: and dost thou touch me afresh?*
> *Over again I feel thy finger and find thee.*

Thirty-six more stanzas he would write, pouring into them his heart and soul and mind and strength, his love for the England that still rejected the Church, the misunderstandings of his devoutly Anglican family, the trials of his vocation, the heroism of the nuns, the gallantry of the sailors, the terrible beauty of the storm, and the mercy of our God who is a consuming fire. No poem like it had ever been written, in English or in any other language.

Father Hopkins did not live long, and all of his completed poems can fit in one modest volume. Only a few were published during his lifetime. Doubtless he thought that none of his work would survive. But his friend and fellow poet Robert Bridges gathered up the poems and published them in 1918, almost twenty years after his death. The effect was astonishing, as if a tornado had struck and swept away all of the stale survivals of Victorian verse. Gerard Manley Hopkins became the single most influential English poet from his era, and now he ranks with George Herbert and John Donne as the three greatest writers of sacred lyric in our language.

Even secular people acknowledge this. And many people have been led from the study of his remarkable language to the only object of his devotion: *The Christ of our Father compassionate, fetched in the storm of his strides.*

૭૭ ૭૭ ૭૭

# AND GOD SAW
# THAT IT WAS GOOD

꧁⊱⁓⊰꧂

"**I**'ll give one tug on this free rope," said the priest, "when I wish you to stop. Two tugs for lowering me, three tugs for raising me. Are we ready?"

"Yes, Father," said his young assistants, as wisps of sulfurous smoke rose from the earth nearby. They couldn't help musing about whether their master was about to descend into hell. The earth about them was gray and jagged, like sludge frozen into shards and knives, and it had cut the soles of their shoes badly. Rumbling came from below. But the master was like a boy sallying forth into an enchanted land. His weapons were his eyes and his mind, some measuring tools he had invented, and paper and pen to record his observations.

Athanasius Kircher, the Jesuit polymath, climbed into the wicker basket. He was in the prime of his life, tanned and muscular from his tireless travels and scientific investigations. "All right, boys," he said, "send me down." And his comrades lowered him into the ominous crater of Mount Vesuvius. But they were used to Father Kircher's eccentricities. He'd sailed to Sicily to inspect the towering and ever-roiling Mount Aetna, and to the volcanic island of Stromboli, which had recently erupted. Then they felt a single tug on the rope, and they stopped lowering the basket, clinching the pulleys. "Nothing in God's world should escape our notice and our wonder," Father Kircher used to say, his eyes glittering like a child's. But for all the wealth of his learning—in ancient and Oriental languages, medicine, astronomy, philosophy, mathematics, optics, and geology—he had a simple piety. "Someday," he said, "I'll build a great shrine in honor of the Mother of God"—but that would not come to pass for many years.

Meanwhile, his fellow Jesuits sent him samples of plants and bones from all over the world, which he collected and analyzed, along with the bones of a mammoth he had himself found in Sicily. These things are still to be seen in the museum he founded at the Roman College.

## All creatures of our God and King

It shouldn't surprise us that many of the most accomplished scientists in history, from Father Roger Bacon (the medieval chemist) to Father Gregor Mendel (the man whose humble botanical work earned him the right to be called the father of genetics) to Father Georges Lemaître (the astrophysicist to whom we owe the theory of the Big Bang) were associated with the Church. That it does surprise us is due not to the Church's suspicion of science, since she has always and energetically promoted the study of the natural world, but rather to bigotries spawned in the self-named Enlightenment and accepted even today by people who don't know their history and who sometimes despise the Church for reasons that have nothing to do with the sun and the other stars. The bone of the mastodon is a weapon ready to hand for dealing blows about the Church's head, and that's all.

But the deep reason why the Church has been a friend to natural science is to be found in Genesis and the Gospel of John. For God in the beginning created all things and declared them each to be good, and the whole of the world together, very good. The first created thing was not mud or something else unformed and despicable, but light—the most immaterial thing we know, wholly beautiful in itself and revealing the beauty of all other things. We might say that the first word of creation, "Let there be light," was like the first word given to Moses on Mount Sinai, "I am the Lord thy God." It's God, imparting a measure of his being to all things; his truth, and beauty, and goodness. Saint John understood it, and was inspired by the Holy Spirit to give us a fuller way to look upon creation:

*In the beginning was the Word, and the Word was with God, and the Word was God. The same was in the beginning with God. All things were made by him; and without him was not any thing made that was made. In him was life; and the life was the light of men. And the light shineth in darkness; and the darkness comprehended it not.* (Jn 1:1-5)

To study that creation in love is to give honor to the Word, the power of God and the wisdom of God, through whom all things were made. It is to seek the light.

### Going somewhere

I'd go so far as to say that without the Church, science as we know it would not have developed. It wasn't an accident. The Arabs were clever and made many contributions to medicine, mathematics, and astronomy, but those were under the temporary influence of what, for believers in the Koran, had to remain an essentially foreign Greek philosophy. They didn't believe in an ordered world, since Allah could call disorder order, or he could call evil good, and it would be so. Their contributions in the last eight hundred years have been minimal. The Chinese were clever, and they surely did believe in order; but it was a static order, cold and timeless. The world wasn't going anywhere; and that robbed them of the zest for making any great use of their discoveries. To study medicine was not to serve the gods, nor to tend to Jesus Christ in our brothers, but to serve an emperor or his officials. We might say, to stretch terms a little, that the Chinese invented dynamite and did nothing dynamic with it.

But the Jews and the Christians believed not only in an ordered and beautiful world, but in a *providential* world with a beginning and an end, a goal, in the mysterious Kingdom of God to which the prophets testify. Those prophets aren't Greek oracles, malevolently hiding under riddles their knowledge of what is going to happen to an Oedipus or a Croesus. They are spokesmen for the providential God, and so when they speak of times to come, they speak of repentance and turning back to God, and of a renewed world, a time beyond time, when all shall be transformed, as Saint Paul says, "in a moment, in the twinkling of an eye."

The same prophets were often common men. They weren't philosophers who withdrew from manual labor to contemplate the heavens with their friends. Amos was a dresser of sycamore trees. Elisha was called by Elijah while he was plowing the fields. John the Baptist, clad in a camel pelt and living on wild honey and locusts, was a thundering voice in the wilderness. Our Lord himself was a carpenter. It is impossible to learn about the good world around us without getting your hands dirty. Scientific labor can be grueling. How can we raise better corn? How can we cure the diseases of cattle? How can we avert flooding on the deltas of the Po and the Rhine? That requires strenuous sacrifice. Why should we abase ourselves to do it, and for peasants? Because whatever we do for the least of these our brothers, says Jesus, we do also for him.

### Another basket

Which brings me to another basket. This one holds a tall and stout young man, so there's a lot of strain on the rope. He's running away from his ancestral home. He has a brilliant mind, and his ambitious father had destined him to be the abbot of the most prestigious monastery in the world, Monte Cassino. That would be a great victory for the family, and well deserved, since the lad was, after all, second cousin to the Emperor Frederick. And why should he balk at associating with Frederick? The emperor's court was famous for its poets and artists and men of intellect. Frederick himself was nicknamed *Stupor Mundi*, the Wonder of the World.

But the boy Thomas had other plans. He was put off by ambition. He sought to join the new order of Dominicans—beggars and ruffians, his father called them. He wanted to set his mind to study all things: God and man and Christ and the world. He was leaving to do just that.

Thomas Aquinas deserves far more than a paragraph or two here! But he illuminates for us why faith and reason are fast friends. He traveled all the way to Cologne, where he became the star pupil of Albert, called Albert the Great for his encyclopedic learning. Albert was, like Athanasius Kircher and like the pagan Aristotle whose works he embraced and learned from, a biologist, a collector, and analyzer of plants and animals from wherever he could acquire them. Many skittish theologians feared that Aristotle's emphasis on the world about us would blind us to the world beyond, but in their fear lurked a heretical deprecation of matter, and not the joyful wonder of Genesis. Thomas helped to save the world for the Faith, and the Faith for the world.

We should call him Saint Thomas of the Creation, said Chesterton. All scientists, whether they know it or not, are deeply indebted to him and to the Mother who fostered him.

⁊ ⁊ ⁊

# THE TRUE HISTORY
## OF THE WORLD

On the Appian Way, south of Rome, there's a little church whose real name is Santa Maria in Palmis—Holy Mary among the Soles of the Feet—but whose popular name is *La Chiesa del Domine Quo Vadis*, the Church of "Lord, Where Are You Going?" It's not much to see, with its late and plain classical front, and its attachment to a brick office building on one side and a limestone wall on the other. And yet it testifies to an event more significant in the history of the world than anything commemorated within the walls of the great city, more than Trajan's Column or the Baths of Diocletian or the Temple of Jupiter or the Senate where the great orator Cicero put down the rebellion of Catiline and saved the corrupt and decadent city for the empire that was to come.

So I wonder what a true history of the world would look like, if we saw things in proper perspective, in the eyes of God.

It's a sunny and quiet day, with not much traffic on the road. An old man and a boy are walking away from the city. The old man is troubled in his heart. He's been persuaded to leave Rome because the henchmen of the wicked emperor Nero are seeking his life. "You must not die!" his friends pleaded with him.

The boy, Nazarius, asks him whether there is something wrong, but the old man's replies are few and distracted. Then suddenly he sees someone approaching on the road, going towards the city. He knows who it is, and falls to his knees.

"*Domine, quo vadis?*" the old man asks. "Lord, where are you going?"

The Lord looks upon the old man with mingled disappointment and love. "My people in Rome have need of you," he says to Peter. "And because you have left them, I must go to Rome to be crucified a second time."

And the vision is gone. Peter rises, and turns about, and begins walking.

The boy is puzzled. "*Domine, quo vadis?*" he asks.

"To Rome," Peter replies.

And when Saint Peter was led outside of the city to be crucified, when he stood upon one of the hills that banked that teeming heart of sinful humanity, no one among his tormentors could have guessed that the city *belonged to him* as it never had belonged to Nero or any of the Caesars, nor ever would.

## A cloud of witnesses

It's not an isolated incident, this martyrdom of Saint Peter. Let's travel across the waters to Asia Minor, to the busy port of Smyrna. There as elsewhere in the Roman Empire, the Christians were hated as enemies of mankind, because they held themselves aloof from such common pastimes as sodomy, infanticide, and divorce, and because they did not hedge their bets by giving sufficient notice to every god on the block, including those gods that used to be Roman emperors before they died by assassination or venereal disease or hardening of the arteries.

A Christian named Germanicus is being led into the arena to be mauled by wild beasts. His is the most Roman of names. It doesn't mean that he is German. His name recalls the laudatory title given to Julius Caesar for conquering the German tribes, just as Scipio was surnamed Africanus for having defeated Hannibal in Africa. Yet he proves himself to be a greater conqueror than they were, because he fights in the noblest cause of all, the cause of the Truth, who came down among us in the flesh. Imagine the thousands in their seats in the stadium, eating roasted walnuts, rubbing their hands or thrusting them under their tunics, because it's not yet March and there's a nip in the air. They want to see that man crawl. They want to see

him beg for his paltry life—not that he will nec-
essarily win it if he begs. They want vindication.
They want their version of a happy ending.

But Germanicus won't give it to them. It's as
if he scorns them and their colossal arena and the
whole military despotism that keeps it all standing from one century to the next. He does not
buckle. He refuses to give false witness against
God. Instead he throws his arms wide and de-
fiantly incites the beasts to make short work of
him. And the crowds grow enraged. "Let's kill all
the atheists!" they cry. "Bring Polycarp to the arena! Let Polycarp die!"

Saint Polycarp was a very old man when this
happened, "four score and six," as he said to the
Roman officer. And just as friends had tried to
safeguard the life of Saint Peter by urging him to
leave Rome, so the friends of Polycarp had hus-
tled their bishop to a farmhouse on the outskirts
of Smyrna. They loved him, no question, but
there was more to it than that. For the Roman
Christians in the time of Nero, Saint Peter was
their great living connection with Jesus himself.
Peter could sit and tell them of the time when
he and James and John accompanied Jesus to the
top of the mountain, where the Lord's raiment
became dazzlingly white "whiter than any fuller's soap could make it," says Saint Mark, and
we hear the voice of Peter the eyewitness himself

in that verse, with its homely comparison. Peter could tell them of the time when Jesus offended his sense of importance—a carpenter advising a fisherman on how and where to catch fish! But when they brought the nets back in, strained to the utmost and in danger of ripping, Peter stood before Jesus abashed, and said, "Lord, depart from me, because I am a wicked man." Was this Peter no longer to be with them?

**But Peter is with us still!**

And the Christians in Smyrna felt the same way about Polycarp. For when Polycarp was a boy, he sat at the feet of the Apostle John himself, who was by then an old man. They could point to the tree in whose shade the Apostle would teach. Polycarp was their living connection to that dearly beloved Apostle, he who wrote those most earth-shaking words, "God is love." Just as strangers in a strange land might be especially solicitous for the life of the eldest among them, the last who remembered the homeland they had left behind, so did the Christians wish to save the life of their good old bishop and disciple of Saint John. And Polycarp, like Peter, initially let them have their way.

But he had a dream that his pillow was on fire, and when he woke he told his friends that he would be burnt to death at the stake. After that,

Polycarp did not trouble to hide, and the authorities found him. He chatted with them, ordered his friends to give them something to eat, and prayed for them and for all the people he had ever met, and for the holy Church throughout the world. Then they took him back to Smyrna.

He would not recant. He had served his Lord all his life, and blessed him, and would not curse him now. So they bound him to the stake and piled the tinder around him and lit the fire, but it ringed him like a billowing sail, and did not harm him. When the tormentors saw this, they stabbed him through and through, and the man's blood issued forth bountifully, quenching the flames before it. The account comes to us from eye-witnesses, reported in a letter from the Christians at Smyrna to the Christians at Philomelium and in all the churches of the world.

### History, on the way to God

The true history of the world is written by God, and so we should not be surprised if it is quite different from histories written by men. That's another way of saying that the blood of the martyrs is the seed of the Church. It isn't just that people are inspired by heroism. Many people were inspired by the land-lust of Napoleon, and the race-bigotry of Hitler, and the fearless ambitions of Alexander. It's that the martyr, the witness, introduces a new thing into this old and dying world. A lot of people will kill for what they want. But the martyr allows himself to be killed for what other people need, even his persecutors. He testifies to the Lord, who said, *I am the Way, the Truth, and the Life.* With every such witness, it's as if God himself has reached down into the world to transform it. And we Christians rightly say, "This is the day when Saint Polycarp went forth to battle and, in Christ, overcame the world," or, "In this place Saint Peter heard the voice of Christ, and he turned toward Rome and took possession of it for all of his successors." Eventually even the historians may notice.

# THE CHURCH
## AND THE BEGINNING OF IT ALL

❦

**O**nce, when I was a young professor visiting my kin in Italy, I was showing a group of boys, with a broomstick and a soccer ball, how to play baseball, when some teenagers sauntered along and interrupted the game. They saw that I was "the American" who had come to the village, and they wanted to talk. When they heard that I was a professor, one of the boys—after the manner of boys everywhere—decided to get his friend into trouble and to enjoy the spectacle.

*Professore*, he said, cocking his thumb sideways toward the friend, *Pietro qui non crede in Dio*—Pietro here doesn't believe in God!

"And so what does Pietro believe in?" I asked.

*Io credo nella scienza*, said the lad, proudly. I believe in science! And then he added, *Il Big Bang*!

Well, that prompted a chat, in which it became clear—comically clear, to the other boys listening in—that Pietro didn't know the first thing either about the Big Bang or about what the Church teaches regarding the beginning of the universe or about what one has to do with the other. But, aside from his scientific naivete, Pietro was in good company. Most people, and that includes most scientists, don't know anything about those last two things either.

## Some professors are adolescents too

That incident reminds me of something less pleasant that happened to me later. I'd translated Lucretius' *On the Nature of Things* into English verse. Lucretius was a great poet and a rather poor philosopher. He was an Epicurean, meaning that he believed that the gods had absolutely nothing to do with man, that all events in the world had "rational" explanations, and that all things were essentially nothing other than their constituent parts, which were atoms of various shapes (some roly-poly, for slippery things like oil, and some spiky, for sharp things like vinegar), and empty space. And so a perfect stranger wrote to me, without introduction: "How can you have translated Lucretius and still be a religionist? Did you learn nothing from the experience?" Such are manners in our day. I filed the letter in the fit receptacle.

Now, the odd thing about his expression of contempt was that Lucretius himself gives the ballgame away in the supposed battle between faith and science. He specifically says that it doesn't matter to him whether you use one explanation for lightning or the movements of the stars or earthquakes or the origin of man or another, *just so long as it has nothing to do with gods*. But as soon as you utter those words, you cease to be a scientist. That is, you cease to confine yourself to what you can observe or measure or deduce from your observations. The claim isn't scientific but philosophical and theological. And if the truth leads you naturally towards supposing that the universe must have been created—if the science leads you to the threshold of faith—then the science must be rejected, or must be interpreted in contorted and fanciful ways so as to muddle the issue. So it is that the zoologist and village crank, Richard Dawkins, has said that if he saw the arm of a marble statue move, he'd prefer to believe that the atoms of the marble had coincidentally, in their constant random motion, all lined up in one direction, rather than to believe that a greater Power had moved the arm at will.

He's only doing what the Soviet physicists did when they first confronted the Big Bang theory. They knew that it sounded suspiciously *like* creation. So they rejected it. Now then, they had to come up with some explanation for what we see about us, and so they invented the Steady-State theory of the universe, which, since the universe seemed to be expanding, meant that particles had suddenly to appear—ping!—*from absolutely nothing*, and to remain in existence as such. The Nazis for their part called the whole thing "Jewish" science, thinking of the Book of Genesis, and Albert Einstein.

## Science and the Catholic priest

Yet Einstein was not the first man to suggest that the universe sprang into its glorious array from a single point. That man was his esteemed colleague, Georges Lemaître (1894–1966), who made the proposal in a brilliant paper published in 1931. Lemaître was a Jesuit priest. Einstein had believed, along with the consensus of scientists at the time, that the universe had existed indefinitely far back in time. But the contradictions between that position and what Einstein and others had themselves observed and deduced—for instance, Einstein's famous formula uniting energy, mass, and the speed of light—led Father Lemaître to formulate the most significant cosmological hypothesis in modern science. When Einstein learned of it, he declared it to be *beautiful*—which was his genial way of saying that it had the persuasive simplicity of truth.

Now, it is important to keep in mind that Father Lemaître *was not searching for scientific proofs of the existence of God.* Nor did he claim to have found such. One step before the threshold is still not inside the house. But he was also not a Jesuit priest who happened to be a scientist, keeping his theology in one compartment and his science in another, and never the twain should meet. That would still not describe the relationship aright. For the man of faith knows that the questions he asks of the universe admit of a solution, because they have been posed to him by the Lord of that universe, who is at once hidden wholly in every infinitesimal moment of time and extension of space, and yet indirectly manifest in the world's magnificent beauty and order. When we approach both theology and science with the proper reverence and deference to the methods and subjects and ends proper to each, we shall respect both the integrity of creation and the transcendence of God.

That means that we will not foolishly seek for a reduced god, a familiar Mr. Zeus, let's say, who tweaks the world from the beginning and then goes about his other business. But we will also remember why we look to the heavens at all. Computers and cattle do not do so. Why should we? What or whom do we seek? Here I can do no better than to quote Father Lemaître himself, from *The Primeval Atom*:

> *We cannot end this rapid review which we have made together of the most magnificent subject that the human mind may be tempted to explore without being proud of these splendid endeavors of Science in the conquest of the Earth, and also*

*without expressing our gratitude to One Who has said: "I am the Truth," One Who gave us the mind to understand him and to recognize a glimpse of his glory in our universe which he has so wonderfully adjusted to the mental power with which he has endowed us.*

## Thou hast made him little less than the angels

I might conclude here, but I am wary, lest I give the impression that we Catholics are rushing to the fore with our arms in the air, waving and crying, "Please pay attention to us! We can be scientists too!" Of course we can be and we have been, and among the greatest—Father Lemaître himself received from Villanova the Mendel Medal for outstanding scientific achievement, an award named after the father of the science of genetics, the monk Gregor Mendel. But that is not really my point.

Father Lemaître held a doctorate in physics from MIT. But he also held degrees in mathematics, philosophy, and theology. And, along with all his fellow priests, he regularly contemplated the mystery of the Incarnate Word, made present in the Eucharist under the species of bread and wine. He took to heart the words of Jesus, "Blessed are the meek, for they shall inherit the earth." In him, and I am speaking about the core of his being, the search for truth was the search for Christ.

The poor addled Pietro was using the Big Bang theory, which he understood even less than an Italian understands baseball, as an excuse *not to think*. The Lucretians in our midst do the same: if they can be persuaded that they know where a man *comes from*, so long as the answer does not have "God" in it, they need not think too much about what a man is. They have the adverb "only" always at their call; the world is *only* this, man is *only* that, morality *only* a social construct, life *only* a certain kind of organized motion, death *only* its cessation. Much virtue in *only*. But the scientist who is Catholic affirms instead, "The Lord, *and all of the world besides*!" He cries out with the Psalmist: "O Lord, our Lord, how majestic is your name in all the earth!"

თ3 თ3 თ3

# SMALL ENOUGH TO ENTER
# THE CATHEDRAL OF GOD

⦿

*Immensity cloistered in thy dear womb*
*Now leaves His well-beloved imprisonment;*
*There He hath made Himself, to His intent,*
*Weak enough now into our world to come;*
*But oh, for thee, for Him, hath the inn no room?*
John Donne, from *La Corona*

**B**ehold two tall buildings. One is an inn for God and man, and one is not.

One is what used to be called the Sears Tower, in Chicago. It's no longer called by that name, because the business in question is nearing its final dissolution, and its place already knows it no more. The tower is more than 1400 feet high. It is a titanic feat of engineering skill, and the most popular site for tourists in the city. People ride to the observation deck on top, whence they can look out upon several states and the vast waters of Lake Michigan below. The tower is gray, glossy, steely, straight-lined, unadorned, massive, and cold.

It is something made by man, but not *for man*; rather for the rich and powerful few whose offices are located in it, and for those tourists who will look not so much at it as from it. It does not elevate the ordinary. It ignores it. It may be a source of employment for many janitors and re-pairmen, but it cannot be an object of their devotion. No old man will say to his grandson, "Come, Billy, let's take the elevator to the ninetieth floor, so I can show you the wastebaskets I used to emp-ty." The Sears Tower is not an ugly place. It is not really a beautiful place. It is hardly a place at all. It is more like a negation of place; it might as well be in Singapore, or Shanghai, or São Paulo, for all of its aloofness from the human world around it. It is untouched by the ordinary people's slightest whimsy or care or love. Some people might call it art. No one would dare to call it folk art.

Now let us look at the glorious cathedral at Chartres.

It towers "only" about 350 feet above the sur-rounding plains, though it can be seen for many miles. And certainly the good people of Chartres, in the 13th century when they were rebuilding the cathedral so that it would be one of the glories of France, were proud of its imposing height, and welcomed pilgrims who would come to their vil-lage to venerate their relics and spend some mon-ey in the great fairs held during the Marian feasts throughout the year.

But, for all that, Chartres Cathedral is a com-pletely different kind of building. There is *room for man* at this inn; and the Church alone could build it. Let's think about this for a while.

## The boy carpenter

We know that human hands erected the metallic walls of the Sears Tower. But we only know it by inference. For all traces of the human hand have been obliterated. A machine did not build the tower, but a machine *might have* built it; its lines have been grooved not by a boy with a chisel, but by machines.

That was not true of Chartres, of course, because they didn't have our diesel-powered cranes and winches and pile drivers back then. But I mean more than that. Every square foot of that cathedral bears the fingerprint of man. And this is not just a matter of historical circumstances. It's of the essence of the work of art itself, of both the Lord it is meant to celebrate, and of the Christian souls who are meant to celebrate there.

Think of the many pious paintings of the boy Jesus in the home at Nazareth. There's Mary, spinning wool on the distaff, or kneading leaven into some measures of flour. There's Joseph, whose hands are skilled at the plane and the lathe, teaching the boy the art that he will use to provide for Mary during those hidden years before his ministry to the world. The hands of our Lord were thick with the calluses of work. He had the knobby knuckles and corded wrists of a man who knew the toil and the sweat, the limitations and the victories, of hard manual labor, of the art of making things from wood—the joists of a public building, the posts and lintels of a portico, a table, a cradle, a cross.

So the men who built Chartres Cathedral did more than work with their hands. They understood that the Lord had forever exalted such lowly work as theirs. That is why they memorialized their work itself, in and upon the cathedral.

"Master Jacques," I imagine one of the masons saying to the chief of the glaziers, "we masons will contribute our share, if you could fashion a part of that window for us." And so there's a part of a stained-glass window where we see three stone cutters, apparently on some high scaffolding, building the ramparts of one of the towers. And there's another place where we see, commemorating the month of September, two men treading out the grapes in a vat, with the laden vines hanging above them. And another place where we see three men and a horse: one of them is holding the horse's head to keep him still, another is shoeing one of the horse's hind hooves, and the third, the farrier, is using a small pointed tool to trim the horse's nails.

And another place, where we see shepherds, those lowliest of men who belong to no craftsman's guild, receiving the first good tidings of the Nativity of the Lord. They will go to the stable to behold him, just as all people, shepherds, housewives, bakers, goldsmiths, knights, dukes, peasants, priests, scholars, washerwomen, fishermen, weavers, kings, and children will come to Chartres, to worship him and to receive him under the humble guise of bread and wine. This inn welcomes everyone.

## The tourist and the pilgrim

No one goes to the Sears Tower to fulfill a vow. It is the object of no one's steadfast love. It has no meaning for one's life. It is a place to visit, but no one can dwell there.

The *tourist* is by definition somebody taking a tour, going round and about to rack up "sights." I'm not saying that it is a bad thing to be a tourist. It is just not at all the same as being a *pilgrim*. The difference is well expressed in the old carol:

> *Come to Bethlehem and see*
> *Him whose birth the angels sing!*
> *Come adore on bended knee*
> *Christ the Lord, the newborn king!*

The pilgrim has set in his heart the Lord of his love. He goes to Bethlehem or Lourdes or Guadalupe or Chartres not for photographs, but for the *phos kosmou* itself, the Light of the World. The tourist may be tired of home, and would like to get away from it for a while. The pilgrim longs for his destination because it is more a home to him than his home.

The Sears Tower says to the lone man, bluntly, "We will allow you to enter, subject to certain conditions, even though you are tiny and insignificant." Chartres says to the lone pilgrim, "Come and enter into the joy of your Master! He too was small, and if we are as small as he, he has promised us this dwelling. For he said, 'I go before you, to prepare a place.'"

The essential tourist is restless because even his home is not a home to him. The pilgrim is restless, because the home he loves is but the shadow of his true home, the one towards which he is walking, day by day. Chartres says to him, "Come to me, weary wayfarer! There is not one square foot of me that has not been the object of some human being's loving and thoughtful attention. Because I am a place for God, I am a place for man."

The tourist turns the wine of the holy into the water of the secular. For the pilgrim, even a little drink of cold water along the way is like wine.

### Singing in the cathedral

What is the Sears Tower for? Making money, I suppose. What else? Anything?

What is Chartres Cathedral for? We might ask that in another way. What was the womb of Mary for?

When Mary housed the Lord, *immensity cloistered in her dear womb*, she was herself the true Ark of the Covenant. Within her living chamber dwelt the New Law, the new high priest, the true bread of heaven. She thus became not only the Mother of the Head of the Church, Christ, but herself a type of the Church. The Church cannot be more or other than what Mary was—the little womb wherein we shall find the Creator of all things.

Chartres then is that warm place like the womb of Mary. It is incomparably beautiful. Its deep blue light suffuses the interior with visions of prophets and saints, of ordinary Christians at their work, and of Mary and Jesus, and the life to come. It belongs to all believers, as Mary is the Mother of all believers. It is where they are baptized when they are speechless babes, where they receive the first taste of the bread of angels, where they are married, where they sing on Christmas Day and mourn on Good Friday and rejoice on Easter morning, where their bodies lie in the coffin, as their loved ones pray for their souls. It is the one place on earth that most prepares them for their place in the sight of God. It is the womb, vast and intimate at once, where by grace they will be made small again, and be born again, born into the eternal cathedral, whose length and height and depth are the unfathomable riches of God.

# A Catholic to the Roots

The fiery redhead is looking down at her newlywed husband, who is planting roses in a garden in front of their cottage. She loves him passionately, as he loves her, but they've not yet shared the same bed. That's because she won't have him unless he fights her stubborn brother for her dowry. She does not know why he is unwilling to fight, and is ashamed for him. But he has left his native land and come to the "old country" of Ireland, in part to set his past as a prizefighter behind him. For a punch of his had killed a man in the ring, a "good egg," as he calls him, with a wife and a couple of kids. He has not told her about it.

"It was an accident," says the friendly vicar to whom Sean Thornton goes for advice.

"It was no accident," Thornton replies. "When I got into that ring, I could think only of beating his brains out. I wanted to kill him."

So there she stands, hands on hips. "What a foolish thing it is, to be planting roses when you should be planting potatoes!"

He glances up at her. "Or children," he says, and she falls silent.

## Immigrant son

If you ever visit Portland, Maine, go to the intersection of Pleasant Street and York Street, where you'll find a bronze statue of a man sitting in a director's chair, smoking a pipe, a crumpled ten-gallon hat on his head for shade. The inscription beneath tells you that the man was born John Martin Feeney, and died John Ford—the greatest of all American movie directors. He was also a Roman Catholic through and through.

My students sometimes ask me whether great art in every genre is always with us, but we don't recognize it as great until many years later. I tell them that I don't think that's so, and that drama is the most sporadic of them all. For really great drama, I think you need something like the life and the world of John Ford. He wasn't a graduate of any drama school, or college. His father was an Irish immigrant who kept saloons and made a living on the shady side of the law, selling liquor in a state that did not care much for Irishmen, or Catholics, or liquor. Jack Feeney grew up knowing what hard manual labor was, and brawling in the streets, and bending the knee in church. He did not fight in the First World War, but he later enlisted in the Naval Reserve, where he served for seventeen years. I don't know whether Ford ever met a saint in his life, but he did meet honest sinners. I don't mean people who sin in a fog of indifference or insensibility. Not much drama there. I mean men and women who sin and who *know they sin*, and who therefore may be found sometimes in a confessional, or sweating in prayer upon a bed of death.

### Drama, alive

"In him we live and move and have our being," said Saint Paul to the pagans in Athens, as he tried to reveal to them the God they had sought in obscurity for so long. Well, the people in John Ford's world, the one he grew up in and the one he portrayed on screen, live out their stories within the great story, of man in the image of God, fallen, sinful, prone to meanness, hard of heart, vindictive, cowardly, yet still showing traces of that first glory; of man, infinitely precious, redeemed by Christ, fleeing from love and yet longing for it, withered at heart and yet ready to bloom in beauty with the least drop of healing water.

Without that Greatest Story Ever Told, all other stories grow dry and dusty. In the true Story, the one that Jack learned at Saint Dominic's Church, the next thing you do may be of eternal consequence.

Lieutenant Colonel Kirby Yorke is stationed with his men near the Rio Grande. His son has left his boarding school out east to join the cavalry, and has been assigned to Yorke's platoon. Yorke's estranged wife Kathleen has traveled all the way out there to bring the boy back. They are man and wife—there's no divorce in a John Ford movie, as there was none in Ford's life; he died shortly after he and Mary Ford celebrated their fifty-third anniversary. The Yorkes are Adam and Eve; essential man and woman; his pride, her bruised feelings, his recklessness, her smothering need to protect. Man and woman: their very vices complement one another!

So Kathleen Yorke stands beside Kirby Yorke, because the men of the platoon have prepared a surprise. They welcome her with the old Irish folk song, "I'll Take You Home Again, Kathleen." She supposes that her husband has put them up to it, but he's as surprised and embarrassed as she is. All through the song, he tries hard not to look at her, and she tries hard not to look at him, but neither one succeeds, although their glances do not meet. There is more electricity in that scene, more human longing, mingled with disappointment and guilt, grudges and nostalgia and regret, than in any hundred movies of pawing "lovers" going through the motions all the more extravagantly lest we notice that there is no heart.

That was John Ford, directing John Wayne and Maureen O'Hara, in *Rio Grande*.

### The drama of the body

No director felt more keenly the holiness of manhood and womanhood. I don't mean that Ford gives us plaster saints, male and female. He did not dabble much in sweetness. He gives us the real deal. There's the bluff Beth Morgan, a good stout mother of six sons and a daughter. She's out in a snowstorm to challenge a pack of striking miners for threatening her husband because he would not join them. She shakes her fist, calling them "smug-faced hypocrites," because they dare to sit in chapel next to him. "There's one thing more I've got to say and it is this. If harm comes to my Gwilym, I will find out the men and I will kill them with my two hands. And this I will swear by God Almighty!"

There's Tom Doniphon, the cattleman who *actually* shot the outlaw Liberty Valance, saving the life of the rival for his sweetheart's love, and letting people believe that the rival had fired the shot. That man, a good but lesser man, is about to be nominated as the new state's senator. He doesn't want to accept, but Doniphon persuades him: "Hallie's your girl now. Go back in there and take that nomination. You taught her how to read and write; now give her something to read and write about!" So saying, Doniphon returns, drunk, to the pretty cottage on his ranch which he had built for Hallie when they should marry. He burns it to the ground, his loyal servant pulling him out of the flames. He dies destitute and forgotten.

What happens when you don't believe in manhood and womanhood? You may have strange creatures, interesting for a minute or two, but what real drama? Such men and women are like birch trees growing in a swamp, their trunks stunted, half of their limbs bare, and rotting from the roots. They aren't where and how they should be. They are alive—sort of.

## Praise to the Lord, the Almighty

And what can you celebrate, if there's no purpose to life? John Ford grew up under the eaves of an Irish Catholic family. If time is liturgical, then we mark time best by prayer and song. All movies feature music; Ford's movies feature songs of the people. Some are songs of Irish rebellion, like "The Minstrel Boy"; some are patriotic anthems; many are hymns. Not the exalted alleluias of the Biblical epics, though; they are hymns of ordinary people at worship, like "Shall We Gather at the River," and "Guide Me, O Thou Great Jehovah." Most moving it is to hear the rolling voices of men singing together—who work side by side, who often fight with one another, who shoulder together the burden of wresting a life from the earth.

Such songs are never mere decoration. They are expressions of solidarity. Ford saw that querulous mankind is only ever united from above. The outlaws become *Three Godfathers* and their lives are transformed, as they keep a promise they made to a dying woman, to save her baby.

The first thing the settlers do in *Drums Along the Mohawk* is to build a church, and their minister leads them in the defense of their lands against the British. When *The Long Gray Line* of cadets march to honor their old friend Martin Maher, the jack-of-all-trades who lived at West Point and became a father to generations of soldiers, they sing out in praise of Marty Maher-O, to the melody of "The Rising of the Moon," while Marty looks on and seems to see his deceased father and his wife, and the faces of lads who had died at war long ago.

Tell me that that could have been, without the Faith! It's like suggesting that we could have roses without earth and water. For the skeptics, I'll end with a scene from *The Long Gray Line*. Notre Dame is playing a football game against Army. The Fighting Irish coach Knute Rockne has been perfecting a new weapon, the forward pass. Marty and his father have wagered on the game, Marty for Army and old Mr. Maher for Notre Dame. Needless to say, the Army team is baffled, and Notre Dame wins in a romp.

Mr. Maher collects his winnings from everyone, including Marty. "Let this be a lesson to you, my son," he says. "Never lay money against Holy Mother the Church."

No more should we.

# MOTHER OF FREEDOM

Three moments in the history of the Church's battle against the ancient shame, slavery.

A young priest named John and a hermit are seated at a table, sharing the old man's spare meal of bread and cheese and greens. "I've come to you, Father Felix," says the priest, "because I believe that God has called me to a great and dangerous mission, but I know I'm not worthy of it."

"Tell me about it, my son," says the old man.

"It happened when I was saying my first Mass," says the priest. "I saw the Lord holding captives in either hand, one a Moor and the other a Christian. The Christian was holding a cross that was colored red, white, and blue."

"We've all been captives of sin," says the old man. "Have you come to me to pray for the spiritual liberation of souls?"

"Certainly, Father Felix. That is the only true freedom, because the Apostle says that he who sins is a slave to sin. But in my vision, the Lord was holding a pair of manacles. I could feel them chafing against my wrists."

The hermit narrows his eyes with a sudden sense that he is about to hear of something new in the world. "Go on," he says.

"I believe God is calling me to ransom Christian slaves from the Moors."

"To ransom them with gold?"

"Yes. And sometimes with ourselves. I see it in my heart, I don't know how. To set the slave free by entering into slavery, as Jesus did for us, taking the form of a slave and being obedient unto death, even death upon a cross."

The hermit Felix looked about him. Most people think that retirement from the bustling world is a sacrifice, but Felix had found it a haven of peace, a life beside the still waters of prayer. He sensed that his greatest sacrifice was yet to come. He must leave the freedom of his cell, to enter into the bondage of the world.

"This will require much prayer and discipline," he said.

"I expected no less," said John of Matha.

So the two men spent several years in prayer, until one day John had another vision, of Christ as a white stag, with a cross between his antlers, just like the cross that the Christian captive had carried in his first vision.

"Time for us to leave for Rome," said Felix. They left in the dead of a brutal winter, in 1197.

### The slave of Algiers

Miguel had tried to escape so many times and in so many impossible ways that his captors came to admire him, calling him the Courageous One. Five years he had spent in Algiers, a prisoner of war. It was fortunate that the Moors respected a man of valor, for Miguel had taken part in their most humiliating defeat on the high seas, at Lepanto, nine years before. Not that the Moors were ready to cede control of the Mediterranean. That was their lake and their piratical hunting grounds for harassing Christian ships and attacking port cities from Cadiz to Brindisi.

Miguel bore the marks of that battle. He could have stayed out of the fray, because he was burning with fever on that fateful morning, but he came above board anyway and fought for his king and his Faith. Now his left arm hung useless at his side, shattered by a gunshot. Nor had he allowed that debility to keep him out of the king's service, as it was on a subsequent diplomatic voyage from Naples to Spain that he was taken captive.

Many years later, after he'd written a few notable works, a literary rival mocked him for that useless arm. Miguel replied, "What I cannot help taking amiss is that he charges me with being old and one-handed, as if it had been in my power to keep time from passing over me, or as if the loss of my hand had been brought about in some tavern, and not on the grandest occasion the past or present has seen, or the future can hope to see." It would always be his proudest boast, not that he had written this or that, but that he had fought in that battle for the liberty of Christendom.

A knock at the door. One of his captors entered, accompanied by a Trinitarian priest. The ransom had been paid; the priest had combed his homeland to gather it, and had appealed to his family, to the noblemen, and to the royal court.

For that is what the Trinitarians would do. The priests of their order, founded by Saint John of Matha and Saint Felix of Valois, would enter a town in brave procession, bringing before them the captives they had freed, and appealing to people to open their hearts and their purses to bring back Christians from the rapacious clutches of the Moors. And sometimes the priests *would offer themselves in a trade*, freely accepting the bonds of slavery so that their brothers could enjoy liberty again.

"Señor Cervantes," said the priest, "I have come to bring you home."

That was in the year 1580.

### A poet looks toward Rome

The terrible war that convulsed the nation was over. Hundreds of thousands of men had died in the fighting, thirty thousand alone at a place called Gettysburg. Southern cities had been laid waste, villages burnt to charcoal, farms devastated, livestock slaughtered, railroads ripped out, bridges smashed, and a way of life, for good and for evil, obliterated. Now millions of black men and women and children had been emancipated from chattel slavery—and where would they go now, what would they do?

The President had called for malice towards none, and charity towards all, but a third of the nation might agree with the assassin who put a bullet in his head, crying, *Sic semper tyrannis!* Thus always for tyrants! The ship of state was battered, its trim and tackle torn, its planks split and drawing water.

That was on the old poet's mind as he walked about his New England farm. He'd been fighting long and hard for an end to slavery in the south. "Am I not a man and a brother?" read the caption of the pamphlets he had published. He was not a Catholic, old John. He was not even, properly speaking, a Protestant. He was that amiable vague creature somewhere between a lover of Jesus and a mere humanitarian. He was a Quaker. And now he wished to write to his countrymen of the hope they should still harbor, in their nation and in the good of freedom for all.

He did not turn to his allies among the abolitionists. The Quaker poet John Greenleaf Whittier turned to the Catholic saint, John de Matha.

There was an old legend that when John was returning from Tunis with his first crowd of ransomed slaves, a tempest struck that ripped the ship's sails to shreds. Behind them lay slavery and Muslim cruelty; before them, shipwreck and drowning. The sailors cried in despair. We might well do so now. But Whittier gives us the courage of the slave-freeing saint:

*Then up spake John de Matha:*
*"God's errands never fail!*
*Take thou the mantle which I wear,*
*And make of it a sail."*

*They raised the cross-wrought mantle,*
*The blue, the white, the red;*
*And straight before the wind off-shore*
*The ship of Freedom sped.*
*"God help us!" cried the seamen,*
*"For vain is mortal skill*
*The good ship on a stormy sea*
*Is drifting at its will."*

*Then up spake John de Matha:*
*"My mariners, never fear!*
*The Lord whose breath has filled her sail*
*May well our vessel steer!"*

The ship pulled into the harbor at Ostia, and the Romans cheered when they saw the banner of John de Matha's cross, the red, white, and blue.

"Take heart from John de Matha!" wrote that Quaker poet to his fellow Americans. So long as your banner is his banner, the prayers of freedmen will speed us on, and saints unseen will be pulling at the ropes.

That was in the year 1865.

### She wants sons, not slaves

I've often heard it cast in the Church's teeth that she was comfortable with slavery, as if enlightened mankind hadn't been making slaves of themselves and one another as long as the sons of Adam have inhabited the earth. The truth is instead as Pope Leo XIII declares in *Libertas Praestantissimum*: "Slavery, that old reproach of the heathen nations, was mainly abolished by the beneficent efforts of the Church." It wasn't enough to abolish it by law, as Americans were to learn. We must really believe that the man beside us, whoever he is, whatever he's done, from wherever he comes, is our brother. So Jesus teaches, and "his Apostles re-echoed his voice when they declared that in future there was to be neither Jew, nor Gentile, nor Barbarian, nor Scythian, but all were brothers in Christ." The Church could not then and cannot now eliminate human evils with a wave of her scepter. But she uses men and women, frail and shortsighted as they are, to save their fellows; the evils she can banish, she does; the rest she limits, or mitigates, or transforms, leaching away the poison.

For the Church does not want slaves. She wants brave sons and daughters, like the soldier Cervantes. And more. She wants men of holier madness than even Cervantes' good knight Don Quixote fell into; the madness of Saint John de Matha, who sallied forth with faith and prayer, and that strange three-color flag.

And that is a freedom the world can never give.

℘ ℘ ℘

# THE "BLACK GOWN"
# AND WHAT COULD HAVE BEEN

⋅⊙∘⊘⟨⧉⟩⊙⊙∘⋅

There's a small town in South Dakota named De Smet, nicknamed the "Little Town on the Prairie," after the pleasant children's books written by Laura Ingalls Wilder and her daughter Rose. Every summer the residents of De Smet hold a pageant for tourists in honor of the Wilders. But they don't seem to hold a pageant to honor the man for whom their town is named, the Jesuit priest Pierre-Jean De Smet, one of the most remarkable missionaries in the history of the Church. That's unfortunate, since Father De Smet was a pattern of courage and Christian charity. Had America followed his lead, great good would have come of it, and many evils—war, the theft of Indian lands, perfidy, mutual hatred, and the moral collapse that awaits a defeated people under patronage—might never have been.

Let's go then to the Rocky Mountains, near the source of the Missouri River. It's the summer of 1840, and Father De Smet, thirty-nine years old, with considerable experience as a missionary, has come to meet the chief of the Snake Indians. It's a meeting that the chief had long desired. Indian tribes from as far away as the Columbia

River had sent emissaries to Saint Louis, to ask for a "Black Gown" to come among them and teach them the Christian faith that they had heard about from Iroquois converts long before. Iroquois converts—that shouldn't surprise us, since the French in Canada had no foolish presuppositions about race, and many of the French and the Indians married and raised Catholic children.

Two thousand men, women, and children have come to meet the Black Gown and to be taught. Father De Smet gathered them for night prayers, teaching them in French, with an interpreter. He taught them the Our Father, the Hail Mary, the Creed, and the Acts of Faith, Hope, Charity, and Contrition. Then he showed them a silver medal, a prize for the first person who could recite the prayers by memory. "That medal is mine," said the chief, and repeated the prayers flawlessly.

The chief became a Christian father to his people. So Father De Smet writes to his superior:

> *Every morning, at the break of day, the old chief is the first on horseback, and goes round the camp from lodge to lodge. "Now my children," he exclaims, "it is time to rise; let the first thoughts of your hearts be for the Great Spirit; say that you love him, and beg of him to be merciful unto you. Make haste, our Father will*

*soon ring the bell; open your ears to listen, and your hearts to receive the words of his mouth." Then, if he has perceived any disorderly act on the preceding day, or if he has received unfavorable reports from the other chiefs, he gives them a fatherly admonition. Who would not think that this could only be found in a well ordered and religious community, and yet it is among Indians in the defiles and vallies of the Rocky Mountains! You have no idea of the eagerness they showed to receive religious instruction. I explained the Christian doctrine four times a day, and nevertheless my lodge was filled, the whole day, with people eager to hear more.*

Father De Smet had the Pentecostal gift of understanding the language of the heart. He could translate the Faith into Indian idiom, walking in their moccasins, and hearing their expressions of faith accordingly. So when he continued his travels through dangerous territory and reached the fort at the head of the Yellowstone, the chief said to him, "The Great Spirit has his Manitoos; he has sent them to take care of your steps and to trouble the enemies that would have been a nuisance to you." De Smet's comment is revealing: "A Christian would have said: *Angelis suis mandavit de te, ut custodiant te in omnibus viis tuis*—he commanded his angels concerning thee, that they should guard thee in all thy ways." The Indians saw in Father De Smet a model of godly manhood. He was courageous, traveling in person to speak to the most sanguinary tribes, like the Blackfoot. He was tireless, traveling more than 180,000 miles, almost all after he had turned forty, on behalf of the spiritual and social welfare of the Indians. He met men as a man; he endured the privations that his guides endured; he sat with chiefs and smoked the peace-pipe; he ate with gratitude what was put before him.

He was a man of profound prayer. The Indians saw that before he took food, he turned his hands to heaven to "speak to the Great Spirit." Thousands at a time listened in silence as he spoke of Jesus.

His integrity was unshakeable. Once, when he'd returned to his mission at Council Bluffs, he learned that his spiritual children the Santees had raided their neighbors the Pottawatomies. He rebuked them: "I showed them the injustice of attacking a peaceable nation without being provoked; the dreadful consequences of the Pottawatomies' revenge, that might end in the extinction of their tribe. I was requested to be once more the mediator, and they told me that they had resolved to bury the tomahawk forever."

He did not patronize the Indians. Of the weakling Snakes, so called by their neighbors because they burrowed into rocks and lived like reptiles, eating grasshoppers and ants, he wrote that "there is not, perhaps, in the whole world, a people in a deeper state of wretchedness and corruption." That made him the more eager to bring them the Gospel, to give them hope of a better life to come.

Most of all the Indians honored Father De Smet because he was their advocate before God and man. In 1843, a few years after De Smet's first trek to the northwest, the editor of his fascinating letters said this:

> *Many of these Indian nations actually thirst after the waters of life—sigh for the day when the real "Long Gown" is to appear among them, and even send messengers thousands of miles to hasten his coming. Such longing after God's holy truth, while it shames our colder piety, should also enflame every heart to pray fervently that laborers may be found for this vast vineyard—and open every hand to aid the holy, self-devoted men, who, leaving home and friends and country, have buried themselves in these wilds with their beloved Indians, to live for them and God.... To aid them in this philanthropic object is our sacred duty as men, as Americans, as Christians. It is at least one method of atonement for the*

*countless wrongs which these unfortunate races have received from the whites.*

When those words were written, Geronimo, Sitting Bull, and Chief Joseph were all boys. The "countless wrongs" and the animosity between the Indians and the white settlers would not end for another seventy years. Father De Smet himself wrote these words in 1841, regarding the "savagery" of the peaceful and honorable Flathead tribe:

*We have been too long erroneously accustomed to judge of all the savages by the Indians on the frontiers, who have learned the vices of the whites. And even with respect to the latter, instead of treating them with disdain, it would perhaps be more just not to reproach them with a degradation, of which the example has been given them, and which has been promoted by selfish and deplorable cupidity.*

Such clear-minded fairness explains the trust that the tribes from Missouri all the way to British Columbia placed in their honored "Black Gown." The leaders in Washington knew it. When the Sioux in 1862 were going to war against the white settlers to avenge themselves for stolen lands and broken treaties, whom could President Lincoln send, at the onset of the Civil War? Father De Smet alone among all the white men in America could make the journey to speak to the Indians. Along the way he heard the testimonies of thousands of Indians, so that when he learned that the government was planning an attack, he refused to give it his sanction and returned to Saint Louis. By 1868 things had gotten so bad that the government again appealed to De Smet, and this time he met Sitting Bull and persuaded him to agree to the Laramie Treaty.

Think of that—the government of the United States, with all its wealth and soldiers, having no one to turn to but one man, a priest of the hated Jesuit Order.

An impressive scene, but not so moving nor so significant as what Father De Smet did to bring the Indians to a love of the Lord. Here I'll end with another scene, among the Crow tribe east of the Cascades. Forty braves thronged about the priest when he arrived, crying, "Black Gown, Black Gown!" and carrying him on their shoulders. They brought their sick to him, and he prayed, but he told them that only God is the true Healer, and that God will punish people who adopt wicked ways, to teach them, to call them to turn their hearts toward him. For the Crows were thieves and worse.

Then the orator of the tribe stood up. "Black Gown," said he, "I understand you. You have said what is true. Your words have passed from my ears into my heart—I wish all could comprehend them." And he turned to his fellows, saying, "Yes, Crows, the Black Gown has said what is true. We are dogs, for we live like dogs. Let us change our lives and our children will live."

It's a message that many more Americans than the Crows needed to hear—and still do.

ひ ひ ひ

# FOR GOD IS LIGHT

⋅◦⊙⊘⟋⟍⊘◦⋅

**I**t's one of the sad ironies of our time that the word "Gothic" now describes an adolescent and antisocial madness, wearing black, as if the whole world were one great funeral, dyeing your hair purple, as if chestnut and auburn were too mild to endure, and piercing your body with rings and spikes, as if you had just been stretching prisoners on a rack. Perhaps all the grime deposited upon churches during the Industrial Revolution gave us the wrong impression. It's hard for marble to gleam when the coke furnaces are burning day and night. It's hard for stained-glass windows to flourish their brilliant colors in smog.

But there's never been a more playful and light-filled and healthily popular architecture than that of the Gothic cathedrals—soaring draperies of stone and glass, their slender exterior supports like spokes of a wheel, nothing merely functional, everything touched by human hands, embracing every artistic impulse, from the whimsy of the mason to the vision of the mystic.

Where was it born? All over Europe and in the hearts of Christians; but if we have to choose one place and one man, it must be Paris and Abbot Suger (1081–1155).

## The man in charge

"But my Lord Abbot," says the master builder, "we can't leave all that space open. It's too wide. We don't have the timber that will do for the vaults above."

"We'll find it then," says the Abbot, an old man even by our standards. So Suger went with his builder and their sawyers to the forests outside of Paris, and they searched and searched *until they found* trees tall enough to serve, much to the surprise of everyone but the good abbot.

I like that little anecdote because it reveals a great deal about him. Suger was the man in charge, the man who got things done. Against his advice, King Louis VI went on the second Crusade, leaving Suger at home to deal with his rebellious noblemen, but Suger was so wise and competent as regent that when Louis returned he named him the Father of the Country.

Suger had been dedicated to the royal Abbey of Saint Denis from the time he was a boy. He was something of an ecclesiastical worldling in his youth, until he heard Saint Bernard of Clairvaux and his trumpet call for monastic reform. As abbot he introduced those reforms at Saint Denis, and he heeded Bernard's criticism of the soul-confusing art that festooned the wealthy monastery of Cluny. Here's the inimitable Bernard:

*But in the cloister, under the eyes of the breth-*
*ren who read there, what profit is there in those*
*ridiculous monsters, in the marvelous and de-*
*formed comeliness, that comely deformity? To*
*what purpose are those unclean apes, those fierce*
*lions, those monstrous centaurs, those half-men,*
*those striped tigers, those fighting knights, those*
*hunters winding their horns?... We are more*
*tempted to read in the marble than in our*
*books, and to spend the whole day in wonder-*
*ing at these things rather than in meditating the*
*love of God.*

Neither Bernard nor Suger meant that churches should be drab and paltry. Far from it! They wanted not churches as showplaces for art, but art as an instrument for lifting the heart and mind to God. So when the old Abbey of Saint Denis had to be rebuilt, Suger aimed to flood the interior with light both clear and colored, and with gold and jewels, reflectors and repositories of light. *God is light*, says Saint John, *and in him there is no darkness at all* (1 Jn 1:5).

### A theology and architecture of light

Let's consider his choice for a moment. Light is the first of God's creations—what does that mean? The sacred author doesn't tell us that God first made the sun and stars, objects that give light. He first made light: as if of all created things, light, intellectual light, is the closest to his being, *who alone has immortality who dwells in unapproachable light* (1 Tm 6:16). Then too a happy coincidence made light the fittest of Suger's aims. The patron of France was Saint Dionysius (Denis), a bishop martyred in the 3rd century. He shared the same name with the Dionysius whom Saint Paul converted in Athens, and with an unknown Syrian monk, using the pseudonym Dionysius, who wrote mystical tracts regarding the names of God and the hierarchies of the angels. That monk's theology, to put it simply, is a poetry of light, of the pouring forth of being and light from God whom no mere creature can fathom.

All of that set Suger's busy mind to work.

How do you bring light into the abbey? Build high walls for a vast open space within. Build with strong interlocking ribs and pointed arches above, to direct the weight down without relying so much upon the walls for support. Brace those walls from without, not within. Replace wall with glass—tall, airy windows. Fill the windows with color. Embed the upper altar with gold and jewels, thought to have been produced in the earth by the fruitful power of the sun. People the niches with saints and kings and queens of France. Show everywhere the light of Christ and his works upon earth and in heaven. Let the whole gleaming white structure resemble a great jewelry box, a soaring gift of God to man and man to God.

### The abbot speaks to us

That's what Abbot Suger thought. Here are the verses he had carved upon the gilded doors:

*All you who seek to honor these doors,*
*Marvel not at the gold and the cost but at the art.*
*The noble work is bright, but, being nobly bright,*
  *the work*
*Should brighten minds, allowing them to travel*
  *through the lights*
*To the true light, where Christ is the true door.*
*The golden door shows how light is immanent*
  *in these things.*
*The dull mind rises to the truth through material*
  *things,*
*And rises from its submersion when it sees the light.*

And it wasn't just that he expected people to make an abstract leap from earthly light to heavenly light. He wanted also, in the art, *to show them how Christ our Light is present in the world.* We might say that the whole of a Gothic cathedral is a door, leading us to Christ by its beautiful and orderly exposition of the glorious work of God.

So Suger ordered a series of stained glass windows, under each of which he appended verses that tell us how what we see should help us to rise from the material to the immaterial, or from the shadow of the Old Testament to the noonday light of the New. Most curious among these windows is one of Saint Paul, working at a mill—of all things! He's pouring the grain into the hopper so that flour will come forth:

> By working the mill, Paul, you take the flour from the bran.
> You make known the inner meaning of Moses' law.
> From so many grains is made the true bread without bran,
> The perpetual food of men and angels.

That's what we are to do when we "read" the art of the cathedral. Suppose we are kneeling before the brilliant tabernacle where our Lord dwells under the species of bread and wine. Its golden panel is studded with sapphires, amethysts, rubies, emeralds, and pearls, many of them given by the lords and ladies of France as offerings to God, to be owned, as it were, by God and by all the faithful, rich and poor. All might kneel there before the Lord. Suger's verses on the panel teach us how to orient our hearts, since even this glorious Eucharistic table is but a reflection of the heavenly banquet to come, and "that which is signified pleases more than that which signifies." The art, the signs, are filled with beauty; and they direct our gaze to Beauty himself.

## A new thing in the world

What was it like to sit and pray in that lace-work castle of praise? Imagine the abbot, that energetic old man, taking an hour from his cares of church and state. He enters Saint Denis, approaches the sanctuary, and stands bathed in light. Let the man himself describe his feelings:

> *Thus sometimes when, because of my delight in the beauty of the house of God, the multicolor loveliness of the gems has called me away from external cares, and worthy meditation, transporting me from material to immaterial things, has persuaded me to examine the diversity of holy virtues, then I seem to see myself existing on some level, as it were, beyond our earthly one, neither completely in the slime of earth nor completely in the purity of heaven.*

Abbot Suger sought the things of heaven first, and the things of earth were given to him in the bargain. He sought to praise God and his country's patron, Saint Denis, in the finest way he knew. Those were the things of heaven; what happened was no less than that he and the men who followed his lead renewed the art of Europe, and graced the world with its noblest buildings, meant for every man and woman and child, because they were meant for God first.

And when Suger died, Saint Bernard gave us an epitaph that was as apt as it was heartfelt. Writing to their good friend Pope Eugenius, he said, "If there is any precious vase adorning the palace of the King of kings it is the soul of the venerable Suger." Let us too aspire to be art for God.

❧ ❧ ❧

# THE HEAVENS DECLARE
# THE GLORY OF GOD

‹๏๛๕๛๏›

The Bishop of Heilsberg lay upon his bed as a man who had much business to do and not much time to do it. His table was cluttered with letters, a glass of wine, herbs pounded into powder, his breviary, an account of diocesan finances, and Plato's *Timaeus*, in Greek. He seemed as if at any moment he might lift his powerful frame from that bed and stride into the hall of an obstinate lord, or down the winding medieval streets to visit the poor. But that was out of the question. So said his physician, who stood before him with reports to make and a question to ask.

"Father Nicholas," said the old man, "have you finished your rounds?"

"Yes, Uncle Lucas. The plague isn't so bad this year, and what with the fine harvest God has given us, I had all I could do to keep the poor from slipping a coin or two into my hand. One thing I couldn't refuse, my lord," he said, "was this jar of honey for your table."

"It will sweeten my last days," said the bishop. "Nicholas, the best money I ever spent was for your education. You're a doctor, a priest, a chancellor, and—a Ptolemy! Now it may take some time before the pope selects my successor. I want you to administer the diocese in the meantime."

"I shall be honored to do a little in return for all you have done for me."

"You have something on your mind, Nicholas. Say it."

"Uncle," he said, "I need your advice."

### Can it be true?

Father Nicholas strode back and forth, hands behind his back. "Uncle, you know the old theory of the Pythagoreans, that it's not the sun that moves around the earth, but the earth that moves around the sun. The cardinal of Cusa proposed it again. You also know that Ptolemy, who teaches that the earth moves around the sun, could not say that the movement was circular, because that wouldn't explain the planetary motions we observe. So he had to devise those cursed cycles and epicycles we mathematicians suffer, as the planets move in a circle around a point on a second circle that revolves about a point on a third circle that revolves about the sun."

"These are matters that schoolboys are aware of," said the bishop.

"I know, Uncle. I'm trying to reason it out. The system seems clumsy. I know that God can do what he will, but there's another way to think of the movements of the planets, one that I consider more beautiful. Suppose," he said, warming to the topic, "we could rid ourselves of almost every epicycle, and explain in a few simple laws the motions of all those wanderers of the skies."

"You mean you could devise a model that would more easily and accurately predict where the planets are to be found? That would be of great use to navigators."

"I'm far from that, Uncle. I don't believe I will live to see it. But I think I can conceive a model that is closer to the truth. And all truth is of God."

"Let me see if I understand you right. You're not saying you have a more practical model. You are attempting to penetrate farther into the truth. Against all we see and feel, you wish to say that the earth moves about the sun. Such movement would have to be of astonishing speed."

"Yes, Uncle. We cannot perceive it, because we are moving along also."

"Wouldn't that motion raise incredible gales? We ride a horse and feel the wind in our hair, not because the air is moving, but because we are moving against it."

"Perhaps it does explain some of the world's winds, Uncle. I don't know. Perhaps the air is moving too, and so it will be as when you're riding *with* a wind, and don't feel it at all, because you're moving at its speed."

The bishop pondered a little longer, with contracted brow. He was, after all, a bishop—a learned man, likely to be interested in everything. "If your guess is correct," he said, "then, because sometimes Venus will lie between us and the sun, we should see phases in her, just as we see in the moon. But we see no phases. She always shines as a globe, brighter or dimmer according to her distance from the sun."

"Perhaps Venus is transparent, Uncle. Perhaps we can't discern the phases. I don't know. I ask, can it be true? I believe it can be, and is."

## Columbus of the stars

"I don't study the stars," said the bishop. "What advice can I give?" The nephew shuffled his feet. "Uncle, I'll be ridiculed for it. Sometimes I too think it's ridiculous. Should I continue in this study? Should I publish my conclusions? The ground beneath us seems perfectly stable, and the sun crosses the sky. Will I make our name a laughingstock?"

The bishop pulled himself up with a look of indignation. "I'd think that that monk Martin might have more to worry about from that quarter. Nephew, didn't the pope himself ask you to help him reform the calendar?"

That was a while ago, and Nicholas had declined, because he felt he needed more time to study it. He was temperamentally cautious, for a man who excelled in everything to which he set his hand.

"Nicholas, my son," said the bishop, "go where God leads you. He gave you your mind; use it. That is why I sent you to your five universities. You've studied law and medicine, Greek and Latin letters, art and mathematics, natural philosophy and theology. You have a heart for the poor, and that alone shows me that you're not a proud man seeking glory. Go in confidence. Who knew there was another world between ours and China? The Genovese sailor himself didn't know it. And now, if you'll pardon me," he said, "I must get to these letters."

And the priest we know as Copernicus received his uncle's blessing and went forth not to change the world, but to set its right place in the heavens.

### Friends in high places

Father Nicholas did not work alone. He'd won a reputation as the greatest astronomer in Europe, and that meant his admirers were mainly monks and priests of the Church—astronomers, physicians, and scientists attendant upon the papal court and episcopal courts, and teaching in the universities, also run by the Church. He had lectured on astronomy in Rome when he was young, and Pope Leo X—the man who would ex-communicate Martin Luther—had asked him, at the First Lateran Council, how to adjust a calendar then out of square, to set the year to be a true year and not five minutes more.

Copernicus continued to toil at his project. The telescope had not yet been invented; he had to amass painstaking observations, and perform excruciatingly difficult calculations without the aid of calculus, which also had not yet been invented. He was careful. But after a while his friends and collaborators began to urge him to put his work in writing—at least a summary of the principles. He did so, withholding the calculations, which he perhaps had not completed to his satisfaction.

Copies of that summary, in Copernicus' hand, were found centuries later. He did not win ridicule, because his readers were not flat-footed peasants staring at the ground to watch it move. Nor were they Lutherans who disparaged philosophy and said that Scripture alone, in its most obvious sense, teaches men all they need to know about God and, presumably, the earth and skies too. One of his readers went to Rome to lecture upon heliocentrism before Pope Clement VII— the same pope who had unfortunate dealings with a corpulent Englishman. Clement gave him a rare Greek manuscript in return.

Then the Archbishop of Capua, Cardinal Schönberg, took up the cause and begged Copernicus to publish the whole of his discovery. Copernicus hesitated. Finally, years later, a young mathematician named Rheticus traveled from Wittenberg to Prussia to drink in the master's wisdom. Rheticus could not be gainsaid. He sent long letters to his friends in Germany describing the system. He teamed up with Schönberg and the Bishop of Culm to prevail upon Copernicus, who at last gave in, bowing to the wishes of so many powerful friends, as he himself said in a letter to his most important patron, Pope Paul III. *The Six Books on the Revolutions of the Celestial Orbits* was published in 1543, as Father Nicholas lay dying.

### Who has done more?

Copernicus understood that God is the source and aim of all truth. That was the common view. His fellows in the Church *welcomed his work*. Ridicule? What deserves ridicule is the idea that the Church was ever afraid of learning.

She invented the universities, preserved the works of the great pagans, and built schools in every diocese, many providing instruction gratis for the poor. She inspired and commissioned the greatest artists the world has known— Michelangelo was one among thousands. Her monks turned northern Europe into a garden of grain and fruit, making agricultural, medical, architectural, and mechanical innovations for more than a millennium. Her main purpose was to lead men to God, not to teach them farming, arts and letters, statesmanship, and astronomy, but she could hardly have done more if she had been established solely for those purposes; and *no institution in history has done more.*

The Church, here to bring us to Christ, brings us blessings for this world, too. All nations are in her debt.

ᘒᘒ ᘒᘒ ᘒᘒ

# THE CHURCH,
## MOTHER OF SCHOLARS

⟨ɷɷ⌒ᘓ⌒ɷɷ⟩

The first sight that met my eyes when my father turned onto Nassau Street was the high Gothic tower of the Commons, where we freshmen and sophomores would take our meals. It was a handsome structure, of great gray blocks of granite, sober, stately, partaking of the earth and reaching toward the sky. The vast hall within, where we ate at wooden tables, was graced with portraits of past presidents of the university. These, I soon learned, were stained by stray projectiles of food sent their way, usually intended for fellow students. It was, you might say, a tradition pasted with tradition.

Like her rivals Yale and Harvard, Princeton had been founded primarily as a divinity school, and you could still sense it in the older buildings, which might seem a natural growth of the lives and the devotion of the people who lived nearby. And once or twice a year, the professors and students would walk in parade, in robes whose original significance they no longer understood—clerical robes worn by students and masters in the first universities, those of the Middle Ages. But other than a few scattered remnants of the past—like the yearly freshman theft of the bell-clapper atop Nassau Hall, to which I contributed by providing a crowbar—there was nothing that held the university together, that made it a unity, other than the name.

## The more things change

We also made noise at night, we students walking down the street or stopping at a bar for a drink. That was not a new thing in the world. In that sense, we were as students have always been, full of youthful energy, prone to sin, free from the oversight of parents, and not always inclined to pore and sweat over books. You can find charming manuscript illuminations that reveal something of the life of students in the Middle Ages. Here's one in winter, and the boys are outside throwing snowballs at one another—and one's a lefty! Here's one in spring, in a classroom, and the window's open, and although most of the students are attending to the lecturer, one of them is glancing toward the great outdoors, and another, in the back, has his head on the desk, napping.

So too there was sometimes trouble between town and gown, especially regarding the more brainless vices, but for the most part the medieval townsmen *welcomed* the universities, because they made for a more vigorous town life and a lot of business. Colleges now pride themselves if they can catch a few students from foreign countries, but back then, so many students might come from this or that foreign country, that fellow nationals formed themselves into unions. Thomas of Aquino, a fortress village in southern Italy, traveled to Cologne in the Rhineland to study under Albert the Great, and then taught at the University of Paris, where his friend and rival was Bonaventure, another Italian, and his chief opponent was Siger of Brabant, a Belgian. They could do that, because even a common person in a port town or a trading center knew more than one language, and so it was no great feat of mind or tongue for learned men from all over the world to read and converse in Latin.

Not just anybody could teach; you had to have credentials. The professors at Princeton were divided into *faculties*, by discipline, a division they inherited from the Middle Ages. Although one university might be known for law (Bologna) and another for medicine (Salerno) and another for theology (Paris), the schools gave courses of study in other disciplines also, by men who were proficient in them. How could you be sure that the teacher knew what he was talking about? Well, the same way you could be sure that the mason knew his trade, and the altar he was building would not be crooked or ungainly. The mason belonged to a *guild* of masters who required from him years of apprenticeship, until he could produce a *master-piece*—literally, the work of art that would show that he was a master of his trade. In the same way, the medieval teachers and scholars formed themselves into a guild or union, *universitas magistrorum et scholarium*, the origin of our term *university*. They made sure that teachers taught and students learned. The masters of that trade made sure that only men who were truly masters of their fields would go on to teach. And—this really was a new thing in the world—a man who was named a *doctor* in Paris could teach at any university in Christendom. His achievement and his learning were honored everywhere.

### But then, some things do change!

Yet in many ways the first universities, those which the Church founded in the Middle Ages, were more public and exciting than ours are. Imagine the scene. It's a warm spring day in Oxford. There are no classes this afternoon, there were none the day before, and there aren't going to be any tomorrow and for the rest of the week either.

But the students aren't wandering about the fields or rowing upon the river. They're all present, as are all the masters. Thousands of people are watching, listening, some of them making records of the proceedings; and all those people will need

refreshment, so there are grocers and wine merchants and bakers and cooks too. Also that part
of the human race naturally attracted to a good
tussle; local priests and clerks; noblemen and
women; anyone interested in the intellectual life;
anyone at all. For it's the great yearly disputation
*on any subject the questioner choose*s, and it's going
to be a great intellectual carnival, lasting a week
or two, however long it takes for the questions to
be answered. Our private final examinations, in
silence in a classroom, with students jotting a few
ill-constructed sentences, are pale shadows of this
glorious and colorful jousting match.

Yet I've still left out the most exciting and significant feature of the disputation. It's simple and
profound. There's *only one master* on the hot seat,
answering all the questions. "Master Alexander, if
the kind of a thing is prior in being to the thing
itself, is it also true that our perception of the kind
is prior to our *perception* of the thing? How is that
possible, when we have all experienced seeing that
there is *something*—say, an animal moving in a
tree, and then only later notice that it's a bird, and
what kind of bird it is?"

And the great Platonist Alexander of Hales,
visiting the nation of his birth, smiles, cocks his
head, and says, "No, the perception of the *kind*
is also prior; but first we must establish what we
mean when we say we perceive." Scattered applause

from the audience; some muttered side-debates in the back; some expressions of surprise; all life.

He's the champion, taking on all comers, and they aren't just anybody; they are masters who have submitted questions to the spokesman for the opposition. It's not what we now call a "debate," with people hurling assertions at one another, or accusing one another of prejudice or hatred or some other moral or intellectual disease. It is not an exercise in flashy talk. The master must identify the terms of the question. He must define and distinguish. He must show exactly how his answer applies. He must anticipate and meet objections. He does so *on the spot*. The whole enterprise implies that the human mind is perfected by intellectual virtues: a thirst for truth, a confidence that truth can defeat error, a humble willingness to submit opinions to judgment, and the solid belief that words are the signs and servants of things, whose natures we can know.

In more than one way, then, these jousts were held in the full light of the sun.

### A university indeed

But that grand coming-together was not, strictly speaking, the invention of man. It was made by God, in the hearts and minds of men united by a longing to know him. It wasn't just that the Church happened to invent the

142

university. *Only the Church* could have invented it, because only what God reveals to us has the power to elevate and unite all other fields of study. That doesn't mean that there is one astronomy for Christians and another astronomy for others. It means that, in the nurturing haven of a true university, the study of astronomy bears upon other studies, and assumes its just and subordinate place in relationship with the handmaiden, philosophy, and the queen of sciences, theology.

When I graduated from Princeton, what held us together beyond our having shared a postal code for four years? No common course of study, no common knowledge, no common worship, no common faith. We wore the trappings of a religious community, but we were neither religious nor a community. We call colleges and universities our *alma mater*, our *nourishing mother*, but it is often difficult to say what potation we are supposed to have imbibed.

When Thomas taught in Paris, sure, there were worldly students and masters, and many a lad drank more deeply at the public house than at the wellsprings of wisdom; but the bells rang the hours for prayer, and young and old alike walked under the arbors or in the cloisters, and they spoke of the world about them, the great poets and theologians of the past, and God.

Those universities could be hideouts for careless and dissolute youth. Such we will always have with us. But they were also, not by accident but by design, groves and gardens for saints.

It is time for the Church to invent the university all over again.

_⌦ ⌦ ⌦_

# FORGOTTEN FATHER

It's a crisp morning in February, and the people have gathered for a joyous celebration. Men with drums and fifes pass by, playing marches, while boys and girls are waving flags and members of churches and clubs and societies, men and women, ride on horse-drawn stages draped with red, white, and blue. They are passing by the home of the wealthiest man in Maryland, and possibly the most beloved. He stands before them on the second story, smiling.

He's a slight, spare man, well into his nineties, but still possessed of a keen mind. A shock of white hair falls over his temples. His countenance is of an intelligent and benevolent man, an aristocrat in means and manners. They had wanted him to speak at their celebration, but he had declined because of ill health. Still, he praised their devotion. "The event you are about to commemorate," he wrote, "must be felt by every individual who loves his country, and who can appreciate the blessings it enjoys. To General Washington mainly belongs, under the protection of Providence, these blessings." He promised to join them in prayer and gratitude to God for a man whose virtues were so needful in creating their beloved nation.

It was 1832, the centennial of Washington's birthday, and the old man was Charles Carroll of Carrollton, the last survivor of the signers of the Declaration of Independence. Carroll was American by birth, Roman by temperament and education, and Catholic by the grace of God; a man who endured much for the Faith, and who fought for the first amendment to the Constitution, guaranteeing religious liberty and free religious exercise to all believers.

## A patriot to the core

Ungrateful man is hard put to remember the benefits his country has conferred upon him, but Charles Carroll fought for a state, Maryland, that had disenfranchised Catholics, and for a young country whose intellectual and political elites were often bitterly suspicious of Rome. Indeed, one of the unbearable things that George III did, in the minds of severe New Englanders, was to pass the Quebec Act, allowing freedom of faith to French Catholics in the north.

So we turn with some irony to another scene in Carroll's life, so crowded with events. Picture Charles Carroll, in the spring of 1776, riding with that gregarious rake, Benjamin Franklin, from Philadelphia to Quebec, to try to persuade the Canadians to join the fight for independence. Apparently the behavior of the soldiers from New

England had been appalling, and Quebec was on the verge of falling back to the British.

A strange couple that was! Carroll the Catholic, a man most pure of heart, passionately devoted to the good of his family, educated in France and England for seventeen years, from boyhood to the prime of manhood, whose father had made himself one of the wealthiest men in America; and Benjamin Franklin, the self-made printer who arrived in Philadelphia with a couple of hot rolls in his pocket, sometimes a Christian of sorts, a ladies' man, a raconteur, of whom John Adams once said that there had to be a hell, because otherwise Doctor Franklin would have nowhere to go after he died. They got along famously. Carroll wrote that Franklin was "a most engaging and entertaining companion of a sweet, even, and lively temper, full of facetious stories and always applied with judgment."

The mission was a tactical failure, but it confirmed Carroll's reputation throughout the colonies. He had written a series of learned essays in 1773, published under the Roman pseudonym "First Citizen," *even though he had at the time no permission to vote*, to recommend the principles of British common law and to argue against a fee imposed upon the citizens of Maryland by the upper house of their legislature, without the approval of the people's representatives in the lower house.

Such a fee, Carroll said, was really a tax, and to tax people at one's pleasure is to strike at the root of liberty itself.

His opponents could not help themselves. Since Carroll spoke for the great majority of his fellow Marylanders, they had to attack the man more than the message. Amidst a barrage of ridicule and calumny, Charles Carroll stood up and proclaimed forgiveness. He and his fellow Catholics, he said, had forgotten their resentment of the treatment they had received from the Protestants. For Maryland had been founded by a Catholic family, the Calverts, and had guaranteed freedom of religion for all Christians, until Protestant settlers took over and annulled the original charter.

John Adams, no friend to popes and not free in his praise, wrote glowingly of Carroll, noting his zeal and his bravery, and how much he was risking from the vengeance of the British administration: "But he continues to hazard his all: his immense fortune, the largest in America, and his life." He was indefatigable. He was a member of the War Department. He spent time with Washington at Valley Forge. He helped to fund the war. Most important, without him, America might not have secured her alliance with Catholic France: no Count de Rochambeau and his fleet, no surrender of the British at Yorktown.

### President Carroll?

Like Washington, the friend whom he admired so well, Charles Carroll was not an ambitious man. He did not connive at political appointment. He was elected to be president of the Second Continental Congress, but he turned down the honor. He was nominated to the Constitutional Convention, but he declined. As Washington's first term neared its end, many people thought that his logical successor should be Charles Carroll, deeply learned, unimpeachably honest, and devoted to the welfare of his country.

But though there never was a President Carroll, Americans owe their presidency in part to Carroll's ingenious compromise. How should we elect our president? Directly? By the people, or by their representatives in state legislatures? Might the president be the winner of a plurality only, or must he have a majority? What method will respect the individuality of the states, the will of the people, and the sense of the nation as a whole? For the president is not just the head of a party.

Carroll, it's said, thought about how the College of Cardinals select a pope—cardinals representing many nations and voting often by national blocs. The trick is to gain a majority of those electors; and hence was born the Electoral College, that element in the Constitution that prevents American politics from degenerating into secret deals among the heads of seven or eight parties in a splintered populace.

## True Catholic, true man

There's much more to say about Charles Carroll's contributions to America as statesman and senator, but I prefer to contemplate the man in his amiable and noble character. I see the eleven-year-old boy in France, writing home to his beloved father—never were father and son more heartfelt in their expressions of love. I see him at Saint Omer's, run by the Jesuits, getting up in the dark of the early morning and kneeling long in prayer on the stone floor of the chapel. I see him continuing those daily habits in his old age.

I see him returned to Maryland, grieving over the death of his bride to be, writing, "I am grown quite indifferent to everything in this world, even to life itself." But he did marry, happily, and his home became a magnet of hospitality. To that home came Lafayette, when he returned to America to much grateful love after so many years in France. To that home, in the year before Carroll's death, came Tocqueville, the brilliant analyst of democracy and shrewd observer of American life. What would we give to have heard their conversation! Tocqueville recorded some of it, noting that the race of the founders was disappearing, and "with them the tradition of cultivated manners is lost."

After Jefferson and Adams died on July 4, 1826, the young Daniel Webster said, "Of the illustrious Signers of the Declaration of Independence there now remains only Charles Carroll. He seems an aged oak, standing alone on the plain, which time spared a little longer after all its contemporaries have been leveled with the dust. Venerable object!... Sole survivor of an assembly of as great men as the world has witnessed...what thoughts, what interesting reflections must fill his elevated and devout soul! If he dwells on the past, how happy, how joyous, how full of the fruition of that hope which his ardent patriotism indulged.... Let him know that while we honor the dead we do not forget the living, and that there is not a heart here which does not fervently pray that heaven may keep him yet back from the society of his companions."

Heaven would keep him back another six years. He died on November 14, 1832, taking Viaticum quietly, refusing food and drink, saying that the Eucharist was sufficient. People all over the country mourned his passing, "the last of the Romans," the last living tie to those men who staked everything they had and were, even their sacred honor, for freedom.

Note: I am deeply indebted to Bradley Birzer's wonderful biography: *American Cicero: The Life of Charles Carroll* (ISI Press).

# The Abbot and the Peas

❧

Consider the scientific work of two men. One of them has all the advantages of wide travel, over many decades. He's sailed aboard British ships visiting places isolated from the rest of the world, like the Galapagos Islands. He's logged thousands of pages of his observations of their plants and animals. He has been in conversation with the chief geologists of the time, some of whom have anticipated him in his theories. He even has a popularizer, a materialist and would-be philosopher who tags his theories with the name "evolution." That name has stuck, even though the scientist himself rarely used it, and though its inner metaphor, that of unfolding hidden potentialities, is at odds with the aimlessness he attributes to biological history. This muddled term will provide the context in which people will think, and seldom clearly, about all things, including culture, art, race, and politics. When it causes them to scorn the past—the land of cave-dwellers—and to deny the essences of things—since nothing remains constant—it is a poison pill for the intellect.

That scientist, Charles Darwin, once wrote that he had no use for poetry. That spiritual organ had dried up within him, along with his sense for the eternal. He wrote *The Origin of Species*, though he really denied that species as such exist; only a flux of states of being, subject to continuous tiny changes.

I'm not going to dispute the greatness of Darwin's achievement. But at that same time there was another biologist at work on heredity, who was dissatisfied with the Englishman's theories regarding it. He didn't have the advantage of travel over the world, or the trumpet of the press. He had to work with the plants he had available where he was, or with strains of bees that he had sent for from other lands. He was unknown during his lifetime, but he didn't care, saying that his time would come. *He* had use for poetry, music, and prayer many times a day. He had to, because he was the long-time abbot of the Augustinian Monastery of Saint Thomas, in the city we know as Brno, in the Czech Republic. His name was Gregor Mendel, the father of modern genetics.

### Peas in a pod?

Father Mendel did his groundbreaking work with pea plants. He noticed that some of the plants were tall, and some were dwarfs. Some had round seeds, some had wrinkled seeds. Some had yellow seeds, some had green seeds. Over the course of seven years, before his duties as abbot severely curtailed his work, he bred and cross-bred pea plants, 29,000 of them, logging the traits of each, carefully breeding and cross-breeding, and noting the results. Think of the painstaking work! And without the romance of the sea, without the encouragement of professional recognition.

What did Father Mendel discover? What would you get if you bred a pure tall strain with a pure dwarf strain? What do you think? Darwin believed that the traits would average out, and so we might say that the parents "disappear" into the children. The next generation of pea plants would be neither tall nor dwarf, but in between. Evolution would be a process whereby the past is lost forever. We know now that there are respects in which a kind of averaging occurs, but that's because of the simultaneous effects of several genes—the word arises from Mendel's research—that individually do not average out. In other words, the parents do not disappear.

All of the plants in the second generation were tall.

"Good for the pea plants!" you may say. The tall pea plant can now raise his proud head above the mere dwarf, which will gradually die out, so that a strain of master pea plants will take over the Kingdom of Legumes. But that didn't happen either.

When Father Mendel self-fertilized those tall plants, something baffling occurred. Some of the plants in the second generation were tall, and some were dwarfs.

"Half and half!" you may say. But no, you'd be wrong about that, too. The tall plants outnumbered the dwarfs by three to one.

"Ah, then the tall plants will win out eventually!" you may say. "Three to one now, four to one tomorrow!" But no, that wasn't so either. *Those dwarf pea plants were not going anywhere.*

Suppose you're wondering which tie to wear to the ice cream social. One is strawberry, and one is pistachio. The strawberry tie is your usual one, but pretty Fräulein Frieda favors pistachio. So you're leaning toward pistachio, but you're still not sure. You decide to flip a coin. Heads, it's pistachio. Tails, it's strawberry. It comes up tails. You decide to flip it again. "This time," you say, "whatever it is, it is."

What have you done? There are four possibilities, if you flip the coin twice. You can have heads and heads, heads and tails, tails and heads, and tails and tails. Only in the last case will you wear the strawberry tie. In the other three cases, you'll wear the pistachio tie—with the "strawberry" hidden, so to speak, in two of those cases, in those tails that you've allowed to be overruled by the heads.

An oversimplification, but there you have it. Father Mendel theorized that each plant carried two markers for the opposed traits, one from each of its parents. We call those markers genes. One of the genes dominates over the other, so when you have a gene for brown eyes and one for blue eyes, your eyes will be brown, not blue, and not some muddy color in between. But the "recessive" gene, the one that is not dominant, survives.

Suppose you and your wife have brown eyes, but each of you had a parent with blue eyes. That means that each of you carries a hidden gene for blue eyes—for the strawberry tie. If you have sixteen children—and God bless you if you do!—some of them may have eyes like the sky; four will be the most likely number.

### A man of tenacity

It all seems so clear, now. But that's what great discoveries do: they open our eyes. Everyone knew, before Newton, that apples fell from trees and that the planets revolved about either the earth or the sun. But it was Isaac Newton who proposed that the apple and the planet were doing the same sort of thing. Everyone knew, before John Dalton, that if you combined one substance (say, sulfur) with another (say, lye), you might get something that was very different from either one. But it was Dalton who saw that certain discrete atoms were combining with others in specific proportions. Mendel's discovery was on that tremendous order.

What can motivate a man to do the work he did? Consider that he had no university laboratory, no large fund to draw from, and no cadre of research assistants. He did publish his results in the local scientific journal in 1866, but his work was ignored until fifteen years after he had died.

We might find a clue in the battle he fought against the secularizing government of the Austrian empire. Every hundred years or so, it seems, men surge up in hatred of religious houses—of anything that suggests that there's something more important in life than "progress" in the pursuit of pleasure, glory, wealth, whatever. So it was in the time of Father Mendel. The government had slapped a special tax on religious institutions, one that other institutions did not have to pay. Father Mendel refused to truckle to the injustice. One by one, abbeys that had stood with him gave in. Only Mendel held out to the end, fighting. The government could come and seize goods by force; he would not sign.

We can imagine the feelings of the abbot when he prayed the psalm with the rest of his monks, *Yea, my own familiar friend, in whom I trusted, who ate of my bread, has lifted up his heel against me* (Ps 41:9). Or when, in his later years, alone in his courageous stand, suffering from the kidney ailment that would end his life, his work submerged in obscurity, he could recover a ray of cheer, when he prayed before Mass, *I will go in unto the altar of God, of God, who gives joy to my youth* (Ps 43:4). He looked to the hills, whence came his help: our help that is in the name of the Lord, who made heaven and earth.

## A burr in the coat

How foolish and ungrateful is the notion that the Catholic Church has been opposed to science! It isn't just that the history of science is filled with men of God, such as Gregor Mendel. It's that the Church, following Scripture, had long taught that God had made the world in measure, weight, and number, an intelligible world, a world of wonders that declare the glory of God; and the man of faith can look closely at that world and praise God in doing so. But one misstep—Galileo ordered to propose his thoughts as a theory (which it was) rather than as established fact (which it certainly was not)—is enough for the calumny. It's like what happens when a shaggy and careless dog rambles through the briars. He picks up a burr in his coat, and by the time he trots back home for dinner, his fur has matted it all around in a great stubborn lump. At that point you can't pick it out. Even a comb or a brush won't work. There's nothing for it but to get out the scissors and cut the fur.

Remember Father Mendel, dear readers, the next time you meet that shaggy dog.

# THE FATHER OF CALIFORNIA

꧁꧂

Several years ago, my son and I were sitting in the beautiful courtyard of San Juan Capistrano. We'd never been to southern California before, we were footsore from walking about the ruins of the mission, and we were thirsty. And there on the grass were fresh oranges, fallen from the tree.

I approached one of the curators. "Is it all right if my son and I have a couple of those oranges?" I asked, sheepishly. "They're on the ground anyway, and we've never had a fresh orange before."

"Go right ahead," she said, and we did, amid the chatter of tourists, the twitter of swallows and finches, the hum of traffic, and, somewhere beyond it all, the murmur of the waves of the Pacific breaking upon the white sand beach.

I have no love for cities, and little attraction to the pomp and glamor of Hollywood, but there I sat with my son on a sunny March day, in the old mission tucked between the rumpled coastal mountains and the sea, eating an orange, looking out on gardens of roses and palms and prickly pears, and thinking that for sheer natural bounty there might not be a finer place on earth.

It was not always so. Let's go back two hundred years and more. What do we see in this magnificent place, San Juan Capistrano?

## Heart aflame

There are no roads, no gardens, no fields of grain, no orchards, no vineyards, no olive groves, no permanent settlements. There are no ranches, no dairies, no stables. Even the dog and the cat have not been domesticated. The natives in the hills enjoy a life more comfortable but not much more admirable than that of their poorer counterparts farther south, on the arid peninsula of Baja California. Their diet is better than vermin and grasshoppers. They are taller and more robust, less fearful of their neighbors. They live in grass huts, not holes in the ground. They can be as friendly as children and as treacherous.

The men go stark naked, sometimes hunting deer, but usually indulging in indolence. The women live in drudgery. A wife can be dismissed on a whim, and a man is shamed by his fellows if he shows special tenderness for her feelings. When food is scarce they raid other tribes. But all the fire of the summer sun leavening the earth did not burn warmer than the heart of the father in the brown robe, who came to teach them, correct them, protect them, and love them with a love they had never known.

The father was a spare, wiry man. He walked with a bad limp, ever since on his first trek from Vera Cruz to Mexico City, when he had been stung by venomous insects, which swelled his leg and nearly killed him with fever. That was many years and thousands of miles ago, miles almost always crossed on foot. He came to bring them the sacraments, and to save their souls for Christ. He was a son of Saint Francis, and he belongs among the bravest men who have ever lived—but how many of those heroes ever gleamed with his greater virtues of mercy, humility, and charity? His name was Father Junípero Serra.

Many an energetic missionary has had a lust for adventure. Father Serra did not, though his journal and letters show that he was a close observer of tribal customs, geography, good farmland, and the characters of men. Junípero grew up on that Mediterranean jewel called Majorca, the son of a peasant. He was a bright boy, and the Church, quick to make use of God's gifts, made of him a formidable scholar. He held a prominent post in theology at the university of Palma in Spain. He could have lived there as a beloved teacher, with his parents and his kin, and their neighbors. He felt no *wanderlust*. Maybe we should call it a *wonderlust*: an unquenchable thirst to bring to lost mankind the glorious liberty of the children of God.

He left Majorca in 1749 at the age of thirty-six, with several other friars, his dear friends. He would never see his family or his native land again.

## The hills and valleys resound

Journeys and missions in those days must be reckoned not in days or weeks, but years, many years. Consider how long it would take for the viceroy in Mexico City to send a request to the court in Madrid and to receive a reply. Or how difficult it would be to haul the bare essentials of food and tools, by mule train protected by a handful of soldiers, over a thousand miles of barrens and deserts. Or that what we now call California was unexplored, so that once a mission was established, there was no easy way to tell the authorities in Mexico just how to find the nearest harbor. Or that the tribes were unknown, their habits unfamiliar, their language incomprehensible. Many good Franciscans lost heart and preferred to remain servants of God in the colorful gardens of Mexico City. Not Junípero.

His goal was to create a golden *catena* of missions from south to north, all the way to the bay he named for Saint Francis. He chose sites near to fresh-flowing streams and the sea. When he marked a new mission, he'd first erect a cross and string up bells—for Junípero, spare of diet, merciless in mortifying his body, was most generous in the things of God. And he'd grab the ropes and cry for joy, "Hear, Gentiles, come, come to the Holy Church, come, come to receive the faith of Jesus Christ!"

"Why do you tire yourself in this way?" one of the friars once said. "There are no Indians in sight. It's a waste of time to ring the bells."

"I'd like these bells to be heard by all the world," said Junípero, "or at least by all the Gentiles who live in the mountains."

And they came, if for nothing else than to see what made those sounds they had never heard before. They learned to see in Father Junípero a man without guile; someone who planned, labored, taught, and prayed; who fed them, blessed their children, and shared their joys and sorrows.

His paternal love often met rebuffs from shortsighted military men. The depth of his love is well-illustrated by what happened to the mission at San Diego. It was a thriving village and farm in the open fields, without palisades, because the Spaniards thought they had made good friends of the Indians nearby. But a couple of the newly baptized deserted the farm and stirred up the tribes to attack. The mission was destroyed. The Spanish, greatly outnumbered, defended themselves as best they could, but their losses were great, and included people who were there only to forge tools or till the fields.

The commander wanted to scour the hills and hang the attackers. Father Junípero opposed him, saying that the Indians acted more from ignorance than from malice. When the two treacherous converts, troubled in conscience, returned to the mission, Junípero protected them. He pleaded his case to the authorities in Mexico, begging for more protection for the missions *and for permission, within the missions, to punish wrongdoing without appeal to the military commander.* In other words, he begged for the rule of Christ as opposed to martial law. He prevailed. The missions were islands of civilization and gentle but firm discipline, where the self-denying priest ruled, not the soldier.

Junípero had no notion of "race," except as a curiosity. He wrote to the Mexican governor that the missions had to be populated, so he hoped that Spanish men might be sent north to work the farms *and to take wives among the Indian women.* Just at this time, unknown to him, American colonists in the east were rebelling against British rule, with a slaveholder writing that God had created all men equal.

### Spreading a table in the wilderness

So my son and I ate our oranges, brought to California by the friars, and walked about the mission. Here were the remains of an oil press and a small oil factory, to crush that most useful of fruits and to refine and store its essence; the olive had been brought by the friars. Here were fig trees, brought by the friars. Here was the wine press; grapes grew wild in California, and the friars brought European varieties like the muscadel; eventually California wines would be known the world over. Here were cisterns for rainwater and irrigation; here was the well. Here was the smithy for forging nails, plows, axes, and horseshoes. Here was the chapel, built of stone and adobe by the hands of friars and soldiers and natives, in that simple and beautiful style that the friars invented, as if they saw it rising from the earth of California, another natural growth in this bountiful land.

How different was this enterprise from anything going on out east! Our humanitarian enterprises even now are a pale and sometimes sinister shadow of the sun-drenched love of Father Junípero. He brought the Indians the bread of the earth because he longed to bring them the bread of heaven, the bread that has all sweetness within it.

He was tireless. Even on the night before he died, he showed his complete self-donation to God. He would not rest before his rest. Somehow he dragged himself to the chapel to celebrate Benediction, and there he received the Viaticum and the last rites. He died the next morning in his cell, a wooden cross upon his chest. The Indians he loved so well searched the hillsides roundabout for his favorite wild flowers, decking his body with them.

"Can God spread a table in the wilderness?" grumbled the children of Israel. *Only God can do so*. For the world otherwise knows no one like Saint Junípero Serra.

ↄ ↄ ↄ

# HERE IS TRUTH

࿇࿇࿇

When I look at the Church, I see a treasure trove of wonders and mysteries to which we grow all too accustomed. The world knows of a million artifacts from ancient days, papyri and sculptures and scrolls, buildings and kitchen tools and coins. Only the Church shows forth the Holy Shroud, wholly unlike any artifact in any museum or in any excavation, associated with an event whose like no one else in the ancient world ever affirmed. The world knows many a good man who deals honestly, grows wealthy, and conspicuously bestows his wealth upon his native city. Only the Church knows of holy men and women who give away all they have to sail across treacherous seas, bringing the Gospel of Jesus to villages they have never seen, and perhaps never will leave alive.

The world knows of many a learned and wise man who is well aware of it, and who complaisantly sets his precepts in writing, as a memorial of his learning and wisdom for generations to come. Only the Church knows of someone like Saint Teresa of Ávila, who insisted that she had no learning, and who wrote her great work on prayer and the mystical life because her superiors commanded her to. But it's as the Psalmist says, that God fashions praise out of the mouths of babes and sucklings, and so too, says Teresa, is he pleased to bestow his infinite variety of gifts upon human souls, "so many of them," she says, "that nobody can possibly understand them all, much less anyone as stupid as I."

She meant that as no more than the plain fact of the matter. Three hundred and fifty years later, a young German woman, a brilliant philosopher in her own right, but raised in unbelief, would open Teresa's autobiography and, in astonishment, utter the words, "Here is truth!" That woman, Edith Stein, would be baptized as a Catholic, would enter a Carmelite convent just as Teresa had done, would take the name Teresa Benedicta of the Cross, and would be murdered, along with her sister, by the Nazis at Auschwitz.

I imagine that the daughter looks with joy upon the mother, in that land where we meet the members of the great family of God, most of whom we never knew.

It is all God's doing, and ours only in and through him.

### The castle of the king

One day, on the eve of Trinity Sunday, Teresa was granted a magnificent vision. She had been longing to be shown the beauty of a soul in grace; and she had been asked to write a treatise on prayer, by priests who knew that she was far advanced in that knowledge, far more than they themselves were. Then, says her biographer and friend, God "showed her a most beautiful crystal globe, made in the shape of a castle, and containing seven mansions, in the seventh and innermost of which was the King of Glory, in the greatest splendor, illumining and beautifying them all."

What can I say of this work? I am a cripple writing about the good fight. I am an earthbound man writing about what it is to soar. But so, says Teresa, was she too. She calls us "malodorous worms," and that alone would cause modern man to turn away in wounded pride. But she begs us also to behold the soul's great dignity and beauty, made by the hand of God.

"Believe in yourself," says the world, whose bloody history has been written by men who took that advice to heart. Ioseb Jughashvili believed in himself, and that was why he called himself Stalin, "Steel." Lord, save us from self-believing and self-deceiving! "Humility," says Teresa, "must always be doing its work, like a bee making honey in the hive: without humility all will be lost." To know yourself is to know your sin. It is to know how far you fall short even in humility: "By meditating upon his humility, we shall see how far we are from being humble."

"Avoid suffering, and do as you please," says the world, stuffed full of time-servers and deserters who avoided suffering and did as they pleased, calling it freedom. But Teresa, fool for God, urges her sisters otherwise, virile in her very femininity: "Embrace the cross which your Spouse bore upon his shoulders and realize that this cross is yours to carry too: let her who is capable of the greatest suffering suffer most for him and she will have the most perfect freedom."

"Seek your own consolations," says the world, measuring worth by the resume or the hogshead. But Teresa says that "perfection consists not in consolations but in the increase of love." We look for no other result than that there should be more of love in the world, and to till the soil for love is to seek someone to obey, so that we "might not be following [our] own will in anything." Love does not seek its own, after all.

## What does the world know of love?

"Follow your heart," says the world, meaning that tangle of cravings and confusions, growing year by year a tough rind of insensibility. But Teresa, the unlearned woman shut in a cloister, knows more of the world than we do. Pray that God will enlarge the heart, says she, "for even in ourselves there are deep secrets which we cannot fathom." The world, old and dense, tells us to reason everything out before we have faith, but Teresa says that our understanding will be most wakeful when we "put a stop to all discursive reasoning," and rest content to be in the presence of him we love.

"Love, love," says the world of divorce, abandonment, dismissal, and indifference, a world hard of hearing and harder of heart. The world is pleased to consider that God, who is Love, will be as indifferent to sin as it is. The world longs for immortality so that it may sin and sin forever. But Teresa begs us so to unite ourselves with God in prayer, that the thorns of sin will pierce us as they pierced Christ: "I know that the torment which a certain person of my acquaintance," Teresa herself, "has suffered, and suffers still, at seeing the Lord offended, is so intolerable that she would far sooner die than suffer it."

### What does the world know of truth?

"Knowledge is one thing, a matter for the scientists," says the world, "and love is another." But when we are speaking of personal beings, that cannot be. To know another is not to be privy to a glut of facts. A spouse is not a statistic. We long to know God, the fountainhead, the infinite sea of the personal. And to the soul made supple and ready by humility and prayer and burning love, God may show himself, says Teresa. Then it seems to us that we do not know what it is to be in the body, or not in the body. "The ecstasy has the effect of leaving the will so completely absorbed and the understanding so completely transported—for as long as a day, or even for several days—that the soul seems incapable of grasping anything that does not awaken the will to love; to this it is fully awake." So says Teresa, who experienced this love, like a lance in the heart.

"When we die," says the world, "we return to the dust, the cosmic dust. How fine a thing it is to be cosmic dust." But Teresa has heard the words of Jesus, that the Kingdom of Heaven may be likened to a king who gave a wedding banquet for his son. It is the secret of the final fruit of prayer, what she calls Spiritual Marriage. In this marriage, there is in one sense no more I and Thou, but only God, as "it is impossible to divide or separate the water belonging to the river from that which fell from the heavens," and so "there is a self-forgetfulness which is so complete that it really seems as though the soul no longer existed, because it is such that she has neither knowledge nor remembrance that there is either heaven or life or honor for her, so entirely is she employed in seeking the honor of God." And yet we are never so much ourselves, so peacefully dwelling in the center of who we are and who God has made us to be, than when we forget ourselves entirely, just as a bride is lost in joy when she beholds the face of the Bridegroom.

I am a man with a rowboat and paddle, trying to describe Teresa's voyage upon the depthless waters of prayer.

## A teacher for all generations

But isn't it remarkable? A thousand years from now, if the world is still here and man still lives upon it, ordinary and extraordinary people will be turning to Saint Teresa of Ávila for her practical wisdom into things that soar infinitely beyond the practical. People who believe only in usefulness will be forgotten, useless as they are. The madness of our day will be forgotten, as a feverish dream. So I do hope.

The Church has brought forth the most admirable women the world has known, and someday women themselves will become aware of it, and return to their beauty and their high calling. Out of the mouths of sisters in the cloister, and married women attending to the sweet duties of a human life, will come, has come, the praise of God.

"Here is truth," said Edith Stein.

☙ ☙ ☙

# THE CHURCH,
## *MATER DRAMATIS*

⁖‧⊷⊶⧽⊷⊶‧⁖

"**S**eñor Carpenter," calls a man wearing the cord of a lay Franciscan, "have you heard what I want you to make?"

"Yes, Señor, but only in a general sense. You want me to construct a kind of cage."

"A cage, yes," says the Franciscan, considering. "But this has to be a kind of prison that seems to be a world in itself."

"It is not an ordinary prison cell, then," says the carpenter.

"No, not at all. The audience must see the cell, but only hear the voice of the prisoner, Sigismundo. Here's the idea. Sigismundo's father, King Basilio, had heard a prophecy that his son would grow up to be a brute, and to conquer his father in battle. So he has had him brought up all his life long in a prison, to keep the prophecy from coming true. Yet Sigismundo has a man's heart. He sees the stars through a small window opening out to the night sky. He hears the song of birds he has never seen. He has been given an education in the humane letters. He has seen only one human face, that of his jailer, who will come and visit him in a few of the opening scenes. Yet he has a soul that longs for the infinite. *You must build me that cell.*"

The carpenter thinks it over. "I've seen a cave by the seashore, Señor," he says, "that was so dark and deep, it seemed it could be an entrance to hell, while heaven stretched above it. Hell, Señor, and heaven, and earth the narrowest strip of land between them. I can make something like that, Señor. I will fashion a door for the scene with the jailer, but the voice of your Sigismundo will come up from the earth of the cave, through a small high opening tilted like this," fixing his hand at a slant, "to show your audience that he looks at the sky."

"Excellent! I believe that will do fine."

The carpenter hesitated a moment. "Señor Calderón?"

"Yes?"

"Will the prophecy be fulfilled?"

"Why, how can it be a prophecy," says Calderón with a wink, "unless it is fulfilled?"

### Leaders of culture

The author is Pedro Calderón de la Barca (1600–1681), the greatest dramatist in the Golden Age of Spanish literature. The play is *La Vida es Sueño, Life is a Dream*, first performed when he was still a young man. Like all of Calderón's more than two hundred plays, it is part drama, part empassioned lyric poetry, part philosophical and theological examination of a few of the great existential themes concerning human life: destiny, free will, reason, ambition, vengeance, and love. King Basilio is having second thoughts about what he has done to his son. He is going to set Sigismundo free to see what will happen. If Sigismundo is the brute he has been foretold to be, then they will clap him in his cell again and tell him that his brief day of freedom was only a dream, an illusion.

Will Sigismundo's reason triumph over his rage against the wrongs that have been done to him? When he sees a woman for the first time in his life, will he be able to put reins on his desire? Can he forgive his jailor? Can he forgive his father? What does it mean, that "life is a dream"? Is all our pursuit of glory only vanity, as the Preacher says? Is it swift and vanishing, like a dream? Is it filled with illusions and errors? Or is this life a shadowy prelude of the true life to come? Is it the prologue to the true play? Is it a vision?

Well, you will have to read *Life is a Dream* to find out. But I'd like to stress something that is not coincidental. Calderón was a devout Catholic, who later in life became Padre Calderón, a priest, and the chaplain at the royal court in Madrid. He continued to write plays after he took Holy Orders. Most of those were *autos sacramentales*, or *sacramental acts*, highly allegorical meditations upon Christ or the sacraments or the last things, seeing all of human history, even the dreams of paganism, in the light of Christ.

One of these, for example, is called *El Verdadero Dios Pan, The True God Pan*. We've all seen sculptures of the horned and goat-footed Greek god, playing the "Pan" pipes, or flirting with a nymph. Pan was the god of shepherds, and his name, in Greek, can also mean "everything." That set Christian theologians and poets to thinking. Christ is the true God of Shepherds, and Christ is the one *through whom all things are made*. We who follow him, says Saint Paul, must in our lives seek to *reestablish all things in Christ*; not just the Sunday dressing, but *all things*: family life, political life, education, art, music, work and play, everything.

There's more. *Pan*, in Spanish, means *bread*: so the Word that became *carne, flesh*, the Word through whom *pan, all things*, are made, becomes *pan, bread*, so that the Good Shepherd not only gives us the good pasture, but is himself that pasture, in the Blessed Sacrament.

You will say, "There's no surprise, here. A priest writes devotional literature. We understand."

Not so fast. The greatest lyric poet in the Golden Age was Juan de la Cruz—the mystic Saint John of the Cross, a priest. The greatest psychologist of the inner life was his friend the cloistered nun, Saint Teresa of Ávila. Calderón's greatest predecessor in drama was the mischievous Lope de Vega, also a priest. The titan of Spanish literature, writing during this same era, was Cervantes, the former soldier whose greatest boast was that he had fought for the Christian Faith at Lepanto.

Great literature has its roots in religion, and the Christian Faith is essentially dramatic.

## The drama of freedom

If we are only dust, or brutes, if we have no free choice, if the world has no meaning, then life is merely absurd, and drama is impossible. The Christian message is that we are dust destined for glory or misery; that we are made in the image of the utterly free God; that God is present and at work fully in every millimeter of space and every moment of time; that time is the moving shadow of eternity.

Think of the drama in the Gospels! Peter hauls in the load of fish over the side of his boat, having set out again on the water, and not too happy about it either, at the instance of a stranger, a carpenter. "Lord," he says to Jesus, "depart from me; I am a wicked man." And if Peter had insisted, what then?

"Sell all you have, give it to the poor, and come, follow me," says Jesus to the rich young man, whom he looked upon with love. And the youth walked away, because his possessions possessed him. The camel could not squeeze through the needle's eye. And if he had stayed, what then?

"Saul, Saul," cries the Lord to the Pharisee flat on the ground, "why do you persecute me?" And if Saul had justified himself, what then? "Do you have no fear of God or man?" says one of the thieves crucified upon Calvary. "We committed the crimes for which we are punished, but this man was innocent." And if his fellow thief had turned to Jesus? "Zacchaeus," says Jesus to the diminutive tax collector, "I am having supper at your house tonight!" And if the fellow had never climbed the tree?

We are compassed roundabout with so great a play of mysteries!

### The only drama there is

Maybe we can go farther still and say that all drama is a version of *the* drama, the one that begins with creation and ends in judgment, whose King and center is the heart of Jesus Christ.

We're in a desert of the American West. A wagon train has been attacked by Indians. Everyone is dead except for a single woman and her newborn baby. She is dying. Along come three bank robbers, rascals rather than devils, fleeing from the law. They come to the stagecoach and see her there with the child. She makes them swear to her that they will take the child to safety. Where will they get water for the baby? What about food? Where can they go, when the marshal is hunting them down? But they do swear.

It's the film *Three Godfathers*, by John Ford, the cantankerous Catholic director. It might as well have been a sacramental play by Calderón. We think that the men are saving the baby, but the baby is saving the men. They are the ones being redeemed from slavery to their sinful ways, and two of the three will give their lives in the quest to save the child. They are errant Christians; the third, played by John Wayne, is wholly unchurched, but he will eventually allow himself to be taken by that marshal for the sake of the child, and at his trial the marshal himself will testify to his character. When the film ends, we know that Wayne will serve his time in prison, and then will come back to a truly human life, lived in the light of the cross.

Hollywood, as seedy as it was, could in those days still produce dramas of sacramental reality, dramas in which sinful man is saved by the True God Pan, he who was the Good Shepherd, who is the bread from heaven, and who laid down his life for the sheep. It's been a long time since the days of Ford. I might say that Hollywood will rise from its place worse than death only if we all remember that in the end there is only one drama—is, was, and ever will be. Then maybe another Franciscan brother, or another priest of God, will ascend the director's chair and call out, "Action!"

સ સ સ

# THE MIRACLE OF JASNA GÓRA

⟨decorative divider⟩

"What is the man doing? Is he mad? Does he want the world to fall about our ears?"

The priests in the hall were grumbling. They were Vatican diplomats, with long experience of dealing gingerly with the Soviet bear. Perhaps they were worried that the match tossed upon the tinder box would blow up the world. Perhaps they harbored a surreptitious fondness for the Communist way. Perhaps their vanity was hurt. But they were in the hall, the door was locked shut, and angry shouts of men could be heard from within.

Perhaps in the Kingdom of God we will know exactly what was said. But there was the Polish pope, athletic, ardently patriotic, exceptionally intelligent and brave, in verbal combat with the puppet general who assisted in the oppression of his people.

What inspired Karol Wojtyła, now Saint John Paul II, with that love for his much-suffering country?

We could call the question foolish, since to the patriot everything about his country is dear; the slow bends of the Vistula River, the abrupt southern mountains, the rolling and fertile plains, the language rich in consonants, the smell of bread and beer and vegetables; the stones of the old universities and churches; the strains of the patriotic poet Adam Mickiewicz; everything. But Karol was brought up in the region of Kraków, near to a town and monastery where something extraordinary had happened centuries before. To this town he went first, when he came to Poland—for the Communists were just as afraid of keeping him out as they were of letting him in. He went to pray at the shrine of Our Lady of Częstochowa. Why?

### The electrician and the novelist

Lech Wałęsa could tell us why. A few years later, that leader of the movement called Solidarity received the Nobel Peace Prize. In his acceptance speech, observing that it was the first Peace Prize awarded to a Pole, Wałęsa paid tribute to the ordinary working men and women of Solidarity, who craved justice and right and eschewed violence. Some of those loyal men lost their lives; others were rotting in prison. It was clear that Wałęsa longed not simply for some material improvement in their lot. He longed for his country's freedom. It was a deeply religious longing.

And that is why he quoted another Nobel laureate, the Polish epic novelist Henryk Sienkiewicz, who won the prize for literature in 1905. When Sienkiewicz went to Oslo to accept his prize, you could not find Poland on a map. The nation has no natural defenses from east and west, and has often been vulnerable to aggressive neighbors, Germans and Russians especially. *There was no Poland for a hundred years*, except in the devout hearts of the Polish people, in their patriotic love and their profound Catholic Faith.

Said Sienkiewicz: "She was pronounced dead—yet here is a proof that She lives on; She was declared incapable to think and to work— and here is proof to the contrary; She was pronounced defeated—and here is proof that She is victorious."

How do you keep a nation alive? Catholics may well learn from the Poles, as our Church's rights are gobbled up by secular enemies. It was never by temporizing, or by becoming half-German or half-Russian, or by going along with the *fait accompli*. It was by courage so faithful that the world would think it suicidal. It was by faith so courageous that the world would think it mad.

Sienkiewicz himself had recalled to their minds a previous time when it seemed that Poland would be no more. It was the subject of his trilogy, *With Fire and Sword*, which takes us back to the 17th century and the Swedish invasion led by the vain and ambitious Charles X. The Polish king, Jan Casimir II, is indecisive. The Swedes have overrun the country, suppressing the Catholic Faith, and it seems pointless to resist. Many Polish nobles have made their peace with the Swedes. They were the sorts, we might say, who want to be on the "right side of history," and end up as contemptible by-standers. For the makers of history are those who fight for what they believe is right, not those who soften their beliefs so as not to have to fight.

And that, in history and in Sienkiewicz's novels, brings us to Częstochowa, and the near-by monastery called Jasna Góra—*Mont Clair*—"Bright Hill".

## The long siege

It is a bitter December, 1655. Twelve thousand Swedes have encamped before Jasna Gora, which is both monastery and fortress. They have all the vanity and power-lust of the never-defeated. They look upon Jasna Góra as the last fortress to fall. If it falls, every Pole will know that the war is over. Jan Casimir will abdicate, for the sake of his people, and that will be that. The Swedes have cannons too. Inside the monastery are 300 men, most of them monks inexperienced in war.

An emissary from the Swedes approaches the monastery for a parley. "Father Kordecki," he says to the abbot, "every city from here to the Baltic Sea has surrendered. You are three hundred. What can you do? For peace, for your neighbors, give in. Don't be foolish and stubborn!" The Swedes add a threat. If the monks do not surrender, they will put the villages nearby to the torch.

It will not be the last such emissary or the last offer and threat. Each new "moderate" who comes to plead with the abbot will point out that the monastery's position has grown bleaker than ever. Some of the defenders have died. The walls are being shelled every day. Food is running low. Ammunition is low. The nobles are settling up. You are priests—you have no business with affairs of state. The young monks are cowed. Why hold out?

Father Kordecki will reject all of these false offers of freedom and kindness. The Poles continue to fight. They engage in occasional guerilla attacks of their own, too, so that the Swedes cannot rest easy. They also continue to pray, and the Swedes from their tents in the snow will often hear, to their surprise and dismay, the sounds of joyous celebration, especially on the feasts of our Lady and on Christmas Eve. That will cause their fury to burn all the hotter. At noon on Christmas, the Swedes hurl into the monastery torches flaming with pitch and sulfur, and explosive projectiles of lead and iron—and this, after the Poles had asked for a cease-fire for the holy day.

## One greater than Joan of Arc

But the monastery is the scene of many inexplicable occurrences. One of the Swedish soldiers blasphemes against Mary and is struck down by a cannonball from the monastery—but the cannon was not aimed at him. The fatal shot ricocheted *from the snow*. Dense fog descends upon the monastery just when the Swedes are advancing to the walls, and then suddenly dissipates, in apparent answer to Father Kordecki's prayers, leaving the Swedes unprepared and exposed to attack from above. Swedish cannonballs often rebound from the walls to strike their own army and that is how their chief cannon is destroyed.

In that same fog it seems sometimes that Jasna Góra is bathed in a strange light and poised high in the air, so that the Swedish shots fall short; sometimes it appears low and close, and the shots sail harmlessly over the monastery. The Swedes tunnel into the rock, but meet down there a venerable old man who advises them to give up, for not in seven years would they be able to take Jasna Góra.

What's most fascinating is the testimony of many of the Swedish soldiers recorded after the siege. They saw a woman dressed in blue up on the ramparts, pointing the Polish cannons and bringing ammunition. Some of the Swedes would then drop their weapons in fear. Sometimes they saw a maiden in white, pointing a sword their way. One time, one of the attackers aimed his cannon at the maiden, and its breech exploded, driving the iron back into his face. Her bearing struck terror into their hearts. "Who is that witch," they would say, "who walks upon your walls?"

### Our lesson

There was, in effect, no such thing as Poland when Father Kordecki refused to budge, and when Henryk Sienkiewicz kept the flame of faith and patriotism alive in the hearts of his countrymen, and when Pope John Paul towered over the flunky, General Jaruszelski. Now we know why Sienkiewicz immortalized the siege of Jasna Góra, and why the patriot Wałęsa recalled his words. The local boy Karol surely knew the history and read the novel, and when he returned to Poland as pope, he too had only an army of monks, just as Wałęsa had only an unarmed host of ordinary men and women, against all of Russia's battalions.

Always we will have the world against us. The lesson of Bright Hill is to keep the faith even when all around us have surrendered. For when Jasna Góra resisted, the Poles took heart and rose up against the invader, and Jan Casimir, uniting for the nonce with Muslim Tatars, mustered a force to whip the Swedes back to their land of frostbite across the sea. Jan then proclaimed Our Lady of Częstochowa the Queen of Poland, and dedicated himself to righting the wrongs that the peasants had long suffered and that had called down such misery upon his nation.

When we meet that woman in blue, let us be able to say, "Lady, be gracious to me! I'm a sinner and a fool, but I never laid down my sword for comfort or the approval of the world." After all, the Soviet Union is dead, *and Poland lives*.

ℰℬ ℰℬ ℰℬ

# MAGNIFICAT®

MAGNIFICAT is a monthly prayer resource that includes prayers for the morning and evening, official texts of daily Mass, lives of the saints, a daily meditation on the Gospel, art commentaries, Faith forming essays, and more.

In addition to Professor Esolen's insightful monthly essay, you will also enjoy our other feature essays from gifted authors who offer inspiring, ongoing Faith formation.

- **Personal reflection** with a feminine voice (*She Pondered These Things in Her Heart*)
- **Insight** into the Word of God (*Is That in the Bible?*)
- **Formation.** An editorial from our Editor-in-Chief on how to grow in your relationship with Jesus, his Blessed Mother, and his Church
- **Faith.** Profiles of non-canonized Catholics whose exemplary lives were motivated by their love of Christ (*Credible Witnesses*)
- **Hope.** Stories of people who accepted Christ's powerful invitation to live in his embrace (*Great Conversion Stories*)
- **Love.** Inspiring, thematically grouped stories of saints (*Saint Who?*)
- **Art.** Two art commentaries to give us a new appreciation of sacred art